Scotland's Homes Fit for Heroes

LOU ROSENBURG is an honorary fellow based at the Scottish Centre for Conservation Studies, University of Edinburgh. He is the co-author of two previous books, *Renewing Old Edinburgh: The Enduring Legacy of Patrick Geddes* (Argyll Publishing, 2010) with Jim Johnson, and *Urban Housing Policy* (APS Publications, 1975) with William G. Grigsby.

JOHN ROSSER has been employed by the former National Building Agency, community-based housing associations in Scotland, Planning, City of Edinburgh Council, and the National Trust for Scotland.

Scotland's
Homes Fit for Heroes

Garden City Influences
on the Development of
Scottish Working Class Housing
1900 to 1939

Lou Rosenburg
in collaboration with **John Rosser**

SCOTTISH CENTRE FOR CONSERVATION STUDIES

THE WORD BANK

First published by
The Word Bank in 2016

The Word Bank is a
community publishing
collective run by
Edinburgh Old Town
Development Trust.
www.eotdt.org

Registered Office:
8 Jackson's Entry,
Edinbugh EH8 8PJ

© Lou Rosenburg 2016

Design by
a visual agency
avisualagency.com

Typeset by Main Point
Books, Edinburgh.
mainpointbooks.co.uk

Printed by
Bell & Bain Ltd, Glasgow

A catalogue record of
this book is available
from the British Library.

ISBN: 978-0-9930544-2-6

Financial support
towards the publication
of this book has been
gratefully received from
Historic Environment
Scotland and The
Strathmartine Trust

HISTORIC
ENVIRONMENT
SCOTLAND

ÀRAINNEACHD
EACHDRAIDHEIL
ALBA

THE
STRATHMARTINE
TRUST

THE WORD BANK

For William G. Grigsby

Scottish Centre For Conservation Studies

In the face of the inexorable forces of cultural globalisation, architectural conservation is becoming increasingly important as a way of helping nurture local, regional, and national identity. The Scottish Centre for Conservation Studies, founded in 1990 and now a part of the University of Edinburgh, acts as a focus within Scotland for research and postgraduate teaching in this diverse field.

The SCCS's teaching activities are focused on the M.Sc Architectural Conservation programme, first taught in the late 1960s and established in its present form by the late Colin McWilliam, with course modules embracing a wide variety of analytical and protection skills and exploiting its historic location in the Edinburgh World Heritage Site.

This programme, and other educational activities such as the long-standing Masterclass series, are complemented by a vigorous research programme focusing on the documentation and analysis of the built environment of the modern age, including such diverse aspects as the heritage of post-war mass housing, the contemporary controversies concerning 'iconic architecture', and the history and values of the 'Conservation Movement' itself.

Current research projects maintain a balance between, on the one hand, an intense focus on traditional scholarly publication (as evinced not only in the present book but in other recent publications such as *The Conservation Movement: a History of Architectural Preservation*, or *Renewing Old Edinburgh*), and, on the other hand, the tackling of complex collaborative initiatives in inventorisation and analysis, including the Cast Collection project (grant-aided by the Heritage Lottery Fund), the

Dictionary of Scottish Architects project (with Historic Scotland), the Tower Block Database project (with the Heritage Lottery Fund) and a range of initiatives in close collaboration with the Modernist heritage organisation DOCOMOMO.

Miles Glendinning
SCCS Director/Professor of Architectural Conservation

Contents

Contents

Scotland's Homes Fit for Heroes is not just for Scottish readers. It goes further than any previous research to unravel what lay beneath a catchy election phrase in 1918. Lou Rosenburg explores and explains the form and design influences on the 240,000 council houses that were built by local authorities in Scotland between 1919 and 1939 and demonstrates their garden city credentials. Whereas previous research has tended to focus on the politics of state housing and whether social housing was inevitable to address the dire living conditions for Scotland's working class families, a more nuanced understanding is presented here in terms of the origins, implementation and location of state-aided housing after World War I.

The main aim is 'to present a broad overview of the key influences of the garden city movement in Scotland'. This provides the bridge between Scotland's tenement housing, the dominant form in the 19th century, and the ubiquitous council housing of the 1920s and 1930s – two-thirds of all Scottish accommodation in the inter-war period was provided by the public sector. The central theme, therefore, is how the garden city principles infiltrated the pattern of urban expansion and built form of working class housing, and this is achieved through meticulous research based on official documents, contemporary reports and maps, and a significant number of site visits. In one respect the abrupt decline of house building in the decade before the Great War meant an exhausted stock of accommodation, poorly maintained by landlords, and in need of vigorous renewal from 1919. There was a problem of scale and scarce resources in an extended period of austerity for the

British economy, and particularly for those communities dependent on the Scottish heavy industries.

The origins of garden cities are well known, and there is a helpful summary of the development with a Scottish twist to show the early credentials of the movement north of the Border. What is innovative here, and unique in the publications on housing in the United Kingdom, is the emphasis attached to tenant co-partnership societies. This was a hybrid form of tenure, as in Letchworth and Hampstead Garden Suburb, which blended the advantages of renting and owner occupation – what these days might be known as equity sharing co-ownership. Occupants were tenants, made a contribution towards capital costs, and because of their investment were entitled to a share of any capital appreciation. From the 1890s to 1914 there were about 30 such societies around Britain, and their appeal is understandable in a political climate that entertained Henry George's ideas of taxing capital gain from property, or 'betterment' as it was called. Not only did the Liberal party see this as equitable, it was also a means to take the heat out of price inflation in the housing market, and lay behind Lloyd George's introduction of a Land Survey in 1910 as an initial means to fund social insurance partly through property taxation.

Co-partnership and its federal umbrella – Co-partnership Tenants Ltd – was to be found in Leicester, Sevenoaks, Manchester, Oldham, Wolverhampton, Stoke, and Birmingham, to name just a few locations, and is another reason why this book has significance far beyond Scotland. Two main branches affiliated to the garden city movement were active by 1908 in Edinburgh and the East of Scotland, and in Glasgow and the West of Scotland. Again a British dimension is shown to be crucial, with prominent individuals in the town planning and garden city circles visiting and delivering lectures around Scotland. This dialogue enabled the garden city and co-partnership interests to have greater leverage and, from a British government perspective, also provided the administrative machinery when wartime demands required housing at Rosyth, Gretna and Gourock.

For the first time we have a convincing explanation as to how the tenement form mutated into the distinctive council housing of Scotland in the inter-war years. The decade before the outbreak of war, when tenement building was in serious retreat and landlords were disinclined to invest in new properties or even maintain existing ones, provided the opportunity to debate the merits of alternative housing designs.

Single-family cottage developments introduced new design options in several Lanarkshire mining villages, and before war broke out co-partnership and garden suburb developments were underway, for example, in Glasgow (Westerton), Gourock, Renfrew, Alexandria, and Paisley.

Nationally a pre-war Royal Commission produced a landmark Report in 1917 and a Departmental Committee was charged the same year to consider the construction of workers' housing. So garden city features which included lower densities, curved streets, extensive squares, varied house sizes and decorative design details each came under greater scrutiny. It is not surprising, perhaps, that the proposal for an alternative to tenement flats gained some political leverage, assisted by input to the Royal Commission Report from soon-to-be enfranchised members of the Women's House Planning Committee including the highly respected Helen Kerr. These various forces have been cleverly cemented together to provide a comprehensive view of the housing sector in and beyond Scotland between 1900 and 1920.

The fluid circumstances of the years leading up to the 'Homes Fit for Heroes' election and the Housing and Town Planning Act, 1919 and its 'brackets Scotland' variant the same year, then occupy centre stage in the book. That story has been reasonably well told already. But value-added comes from the spatial understanding that is provided by mapping the 300 local authority developments produced under the 1919 legislation. Some were small – a few houses only compared to the 1,500 built by Glasgow City Council, where the roll call of names is instantly recognised by locals – Riddrie, Govanhill, Craighton, Elder Park and Mosspark in Glasgow. Elsewhere, Chesser, Hutchison, and Northfield in Edinburgh; Logie in Dundee; and Torry in Aberdeen. Housing types varied from single-family cottages to 4-in-a-block flats and in some cases to free-standing 3-storey tenements, with distinctive local variants within the smaller settlements in rural areas. Sometimes firms were involved directly in setting up public utility societies, as at Kinlochleven to support the British Aluminium Company workforce, or in Fife to house workers employed by the Burntisland Shipbuilding Company. Here Rosenburg revises our understanding of early social housing by showing how public utility societies took the initiative to obtain a 30 per cent lump sum from the state to fund much needed housing, as did The Scottish Veterans' Garden City Association to house the war wounded by completing 220 houses in 20 different developments.

This is no rose-tinted account of the garden city movement, nor of the promises associated with the election of 1918. Indeed, Lou Rosenburg recognises the power of the City Councils, the austerity of the 1920s, and the depression of the 1930s meant that the housing needs were beyond the capacity of the garden city and public utility society endeavours. And when the rate of interest dropped to historic lows from 1932, private sector projects by Mactaggart and Mickel, Miller, and others cloned bungaloid developments for in-work clerks and middle classes of the city and colonised another segment of the market. His conclusion, however, is pertinent to an understanding of Scottish towns and cities today: 'The local authority developments that stemmed from the 1919 Act resulted in a striking transition in the built form of working class housing in Scotland'. Many of these developments, considered to be of 'outstanding quality' by the Scottish Architectural Advisory Committee in 1935, also 'were seen as genuine achievements and worthy symbols of the political promises that were made to deliver 'Homes Fit for Heroes'. Many a politician since would wish for such an epitaph.

Richard Rodger
Professor of Economic & Social History
University of Edinburgh

Acknowledgements

The background research for this book began in earnest during 2006, following a query from Julian Holder who was then a colleague at Edinburgh College of Art. Julian asked if I knew of something that provided a broad account of the early influences of the garden city movement in Scotland. Upon reflection, I was unable to think of a coherent overview of the Scottish experience from 1900 to 1939, and we agreed to try to produce one on a collaborative basis.

In September 2007, we presented our 'work in progress' at the first session of a 2-stage conference sponsored by the Paul Mellon Centre for the Study of British Art with the theme 'Fruits of Exchange: England, Scotland and Architecture'. At this initial session held at Edinburgh College of Art, the various contributions focused on English architectural influences in Scotland. The response to our talk was generally positive and for a time the background research continued. At the end of academic year 2007-08, however, Julian decided to take up a new post in Manchester and it proved difficult to continue the work on a collaborative basis.

Over the next three years, I persevered with the background research but was still uncertain about the type of end product that might emerge. Fortunately, from time to time, I was able to discuss the work with Miles Glendinning and Richard Rodger and gradually began to see the potential for a book that could be written for a general audience. Without the sustained interest and helpful advice of these two distinguished authors, I might well have abandoned the project altogether.

The rate of progress increased significantly in 2011 when John Rosser

Acknowledgements

– a long-time friend who worked in architecture and planning – offered his services on a purely voluntary basis. He was keen to help with small areas of research, site visits and photographs, and the search for appropriate visual material. His advice on issues relating to architectural design and site planning was also extremely valuable in framing the key arguments presented in the text. John Rosser's contributions, and the energetic support and good-humoured prodding of managing editor Sean Bradley, played a vital part in bringing this project to fruition.

I am also grateful for the advice and support given by many others, including Carly Bremner, Ian Campbell, Rob Cowan, Elizabeth Cumming, Hector Currie, the late Tom Duncan, Chris Fleet, Leslie Forsyth, Eric Grosso, Ann Hamilton, Jim Johnson, Katy Lock, Peter Minshall, Jonathan Molloy, Iain Paterson, Graeme Purves, John Reiach, Jennie Renton, Peter Robinson, Mike Thornley, Sue Thornley, Rachel Travers, Ola Uduku, Graham Urquhart and the late David Witham. In addition, thanks are due to two organisations that were especially generous in making available graphic material for inclusion in this book – Letchworth Garden City Heritage Foundation and the Town and Country Planning Association

Any errors of fact, interpretation or omission are, of course, my sole responsibility.

Lou Rosenburg
Honorary Fellow
Scottish Centre for Conservation Studies
University of Edinburgh
May 2016

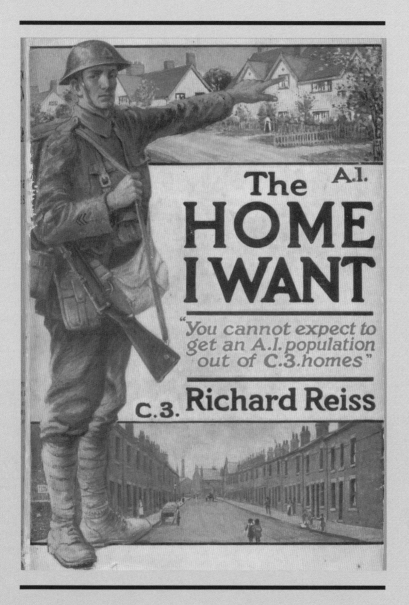

PREVIOUS PAGE: Cover illustration for book by Capt. Richard Reiss, distinguished veteran of World War 1 and garden city enthusiast.

BELOW: 'The Veteran's Dream', watercolour by an unidentified artist which was to promote the work of The Scottish Veterans' Garden City Association.

THE VETERAN'S DREAM.

The political catchphrases 'A Land Fit for Heroes to Live In' and 'Homes Fit for Heroes' were used first in Britain during the closing stages of World War One (WW1), once victory was assured and a general election was clearly on the horizon. During the electoral campaign of 1918, these rallying cries raised awareness of the need for national policies to promote social reconstruction and better living conditions for ordinary people. After the election, the Coalition Government introduced major changes in housing policy in an effort to fulfil campaign promises and to ease the conditions of shortage that existed in many parts of Britain. Over the next decade, the main objective of national housing policy was to expand the general supply of accommodation by building lower density dwellings for working class families. These efforts were strongly influenced by the ideas and experience of the garden city movement.

The desired forms of accommodation were intended to set new standards for working class housing across the whole of Britain. In order to generate the necessary volume of new construction, local authorities were given a statutory duty to ensure that housing needs in their areas were being addressed. During the early 1920s, in difficult economic conditions, local authorities were asked to take the lead in building well designed working class dwellings along garden city lines. Within Scotland's larger cities and towns, this type of accommodation provided a striking contrast to the traditional pattern of tenement living. The new council housing developments introduced significant changes in the physical character of urban expansion and the range of housing options available to better off working class households.

In recent years, the attention given to the centenary of WW1 has highlighted both the 'Homes Fit for Heroes' campaign and the persistence of deplorable living conditions on the home front. Somewhat surprisingly, the ideas and early experience of the garden city movement have also influenced current policy debates about how best to meet the continuing housing pressures in the south of England. The notion of creating several self-contained garden cities in key locations has been gathering broad political support as a potential means of containing urban sprawl and avoiding further destruction of the countryside.

The main aim of this book is to present a broad overview of the influences of the garden city movement in Scotland from 1900 to 1939, with particular reference to the built form of working class housing and the general pattern of urban expansion.

There are numerous contributions in the literature focusing on the early history of the mainstream garden city movement, but these accounts tend to say very little about the wider Scottish experience. Some attention is normally given to specific projects north of the Border, such as the wartime housing built at Gretna and Rosyth, which are regarded as noteworthy from a British perspective. There is also a more limited Scottish literature on the subject which to date has focused primarily upon local and regional aspects of the story rather than the overall picture. This book is therefore intended to examine the Scottish dimension of the early garden city movement and to assess its influence across the whole of Scotland.

When considering the legacy of the early garden city movement, it is important to recognise the limitations of what was actually achieved between 1900 and 1939. Throughout Britain only 2 new settlements were directly inspired by Ebenezer Howard's vision for garden cities. Both were located in the southeast of England, at Letchworth and Welwyn Garden City. The style of housing favoured by the garden city movement did have a major influence on the pattern of suburban development, but many of the committed garden city enthusiasts regarded the sprawling suburbs as a poor substitute for properly planned self-contained communities.

The following passage from the writings of Stephen Ward acknowledges both the limited progress in building genuine garden cities and the broader impact on the general pattern of housing provision:

[Ebenezer] Howard's grand vision of a peaceful path to real (social) reform was nowhere fulfilled. Many parts of the world ... were deeply touched by his ideas. Yet the direct impact of what ... were his most cherished ideas was quite small. The two garden cities at Letchworth and Welwyn were the best embodiments of his thinking. They were by any standards remarkable achievements. But there were many compromises ... crucially ... the central principle of collective community ownership of the land on which the garden cities were built was never realised in the way he hoped. The companies established to build the garden cities were scarcely models of stakeholder co-operation... This was not, of course, the whole story. Very quickly, the garden city came to be understood in a more limited sense, as an urban planning model to reform the spatial arrangement of social and economic life... It was the residential environments and site layouts created by Raymond Unwin, Barry Parker, and those who followed that became the most specific direct legacy of the garden city [movement].[1]

1. Steven V. Ward, 'The Howard legacy' in K. C. Parsons and D. Schuyler (eds.), *From Garden City to Green City* (Baltimore and London, 2002), pp. 223-4.

Stephen Ward's reflections have particular resonance for an understanding of the Scottish experience. Although various attempts were made to promote a full-scale garden city in Scotland, nothing materialised on the ground between 1900 and 1939 which conformed closely to Howard's original vision. The promotion of garden city ideas did, however, have a marked influence on the design and layout of working class housing during this period, particularly on the periphery of larger cities and towns. This process began on a small scale before 1914, primarily through the efforts of voluntary bodies that were committed to providing a viable alternative to tenement accommodation for skilled workers and their families. During the course of WW1, the volume of garden city style housing was expanded significantly in conjunction with central government efforts to ensure that an adequate supply of suitable accommodation was available for incoming defence workers. After the Armistice, lower density cottage developments were built on an even larger scale throughout Scotland, initially mainly by local authorities under central government supervision, using the newly enacted statutory framework of the Housing and Town Planning (Scotland) Act of 1919.

Before considering the influences of the garden city movement in

Scotland from 1900 to 1939, it is necessary to set the scene with two types of contextual discussion. The first 2 chapters that follow are concerned with the evolution of the Scottish tenement tradition and the early development of the mainstream garden city movement. Taken together, the remaining 5 chapters present an overview of the Scottish dimension of the garden city movement with particular reference to the impact on the built form of working class housing. The overview is based partly on the published work of other authors and partly on original research and site visits.

Scotland's Tenement Tradition

PREVIOUS PAGE: 'Canongate
Washing', artist's impression
of tenement living in the Old
Town of Edinburgh, by Ernest S.
Lumsden (c. 1934).

BELOW: Edinburgh's Lawnmarket,
cradle of the Scottish tenement.
(Photo: John Reiach)

Tenement building in Scotland is an ancient tradition dating back to medieval times. As noted by Frank Walker, this vertical form of purpose-built flats has accommodated a wide range of income groups over the centuries:

1. Frank Arneil Walker, 'The Glasgow grid' in T. A. Markus (ed.), *Order and Space in Society* (Edinburgh, 1982), p. 156.

> The tenement . . . has a long record. It is the predominating building type in the fabric of Scottish towns. From medieval times to the present it has proved acceptable . . . to all but the most elevated strata of society. The tenement has accommodated proletarian and professional alike, social distinctions being achieved first by vertical gradations within a single building block and later by district locations within the expanding city.[1]

The origins of Scottish tenements have long been debated in the literature. Whether the tenement tradition can be best explained by indigenous factors, such as the high cost of land and the backward state of Scotland's economy, or by external factors such as the influence of Continental living patterns, has never been fully resolved. How the tradition of tenement building became common practice in various parts of Scotland has also remained a matter of conjecture.

In the British context, Scotland's tenement tradition is usually regarded as an anomaly. The construction of higher density flats is a relatively recent phenomenon in English cities, which is often associated with the development of philanthropic housing from the middle decades of the 19th century. Purely commercial forms of flat building tended to be concentrated in London, Northumberland and Tyneside. In many English cities, the dominant form of artisan housing evolved from 'back-to-back' houses to single-family terraced cottages during this period.

When viewed in a European context, Scotland's tenement tradition seems much nearer to the norm since many Continental cities also have a long standing pattern of vertical living. Not surprisingly, numerous authors have drawn attention to Scotland's historic links with France as a possible explanation for tenement building north of the Border. Before considering the various influences on the early development of tenements in Scotland, it is necessary to clarify what is meant by a 'tenement' in the Scottish context. This term generally refers to a pur-pose-built, walk-up structure, with self-contained spaces on the upper floors that were originally intended for residential use. Peter Robinson has suggested the following working definition:

> The popular understanding of the term 'tenement' in Scotland is a massive Victorian or Edwardian stone structure of between 3 and 5 storeys in height, containing up to 20 or so flats, These flats are reached by a common passage, universally referred to as a 'close' and a 'stair'.[2]

In other parts of the United Kingdom, the term is used differently to refer to what Scots would call a 'sub-divided' or 'made-down' house. This type of property would have been built originally as a single large house for a relatively prosperous family, and later converted into a warren of smaller spaces for a much poorer section of the population.[3]

PRE-INDUSTRIAL ORIGINS

The inception of tenement living in Scotland was closely associated with the medieval development of Edinburgh. Once the vertical pattern of accommodation had become firmly established in Edinburgh about 500 years ago, it gradually spread to other Scottish burghs. Various indigenous factors appear to have influenced this form of building, particularly on restricted sites. According to Richard Rodger,

2. Peter J. Robinson, 'Tenements: a pre-industrial urban tradition', *ROSC Review of Scottish Culture*, No. 1, 1984, p. 52.
3. Ibid.

the introduction of tenement building in Scotland was likely to have resulted from the following combination of circumstances:[4]

- *Adverse climatic conditions* – in the damp Scottish climate, living off the ground was especially advantageous in severe winter weather.

- *Availability of suitable materials* – an abundance of good stone made it feasible to build relatively large vertical structures comprising separate self-contained dwellings.

- *Need for security* – in certain cases, such as Edinburgh and Stirling, walled towns evolved in response to prolonged Anglo-Scottish hostilities, and over time these fortifications tended to inhibit outward expansion, to inflate land prices, and to encourage vertical forms of redevelopment on highly accessible sites.

- *Mercantile privilege* – medieval Scottish burghs were privileged trading enclaves with clearly defined boundaries, and where walls had not been built for defence purposes there would still have been deep ditches and earthen mounds to constrain outward expansion.

- *Economic underdevelopment* – given the backward state of the medieval Scottish economy, the living standards of wealthier merchants in Scotland were much less luxurious than the conditions enjoyed by better-off merchants in England, Spain, Portugal, Germany and Flanders, and in these circumstances many of Scotland's merchants appear to have made their homes in comparatively modest flats rather than elegant town houses.

In these conditions, the conventional arrangements for living above ground evolved over time. The earliest types of flatted accommodation were usually 2-storey structures. Within the Scottish Borders and Northumberland, for security reasons, farm buildings were constructed with domestic living space on the upper floor accessed by a removable

4. Richard Rodger, 'The invisible hand – market forces, housing and the urban form in Victorian cities' in D. Fraser and A. Sutcliffe (eds.), *The Pursuit of Urban History* (London, 1983), pp. 190-211.

RIGHT: New Lane, Newhaven.

Newhaven.
New Lane.

5. Robinson, 'Tenements: a pre-industrial urban tradition', p. 54.
6. John G. Harrison, 'Wooden-fronted houses and forestairs in early modern Scotland', *Architectural Heritage* IX, 1998, p. 78.
7. Robinson, 'Tenements: a pre-industrial tradition', pp. 56-7.

ladder.[5] In Scottish fishing villages, and in other places where cottage industries were expanding, 2-storey structures appeared with work or storage space on one level and living quarters on the other. Within the larger settlements, as commercial activities expanded along the main thoroughfares, local merchants often lived above their shops, in a flat that was accessed directly from the street via a forestair.[6]

The early development of Edinburgh was influenced by the natural features of the site and the official boundaries of the Royal Burgh. When the settlement was originally established at the start of the 12th century, growth could be readily accommodated through lateral expansion of built-up areas. Two centuries later, the town walls that had been constructed for defence purposes were seriously constraining the pattern of outward growth. By the start of the 15th century, Edinburgh had become the permanent seat of the Scottish Government and from 1535 the Court of Sessions met regularly in Edinburgh. Many of Scotland's prominent noblemen, landowners, judges and lawyers found it essential to be based in Edinburgh for at least part of the year. In effect, these elite part-time residents competed with the town's wealthier merchants for the most desirable locations along the Royal Mile.[7]

With the growth of commerce and civic functions, and the rise in population, the potential supply of land for new development within the city walls became increasingly scarce. Expansion in a northerly direction was severely constrained by the position of the Nor' Loch, located on

TOP LEFT: Black Bull Close, Port Glasgow.

TOP RIGHT: Mince Collop Close, Greenock.

LEFT: High Street, Prestopans.

the site which now contains Princes Street Gardens. To the south and west, both steep topography and the prevailing pattern of land ownership acted as major barriers to new forms of lateral development. In terms of physical conditions, more obvious opportunities were located to the east, but this land formed part of the separate Burgh of Canongate. In the face of these various constraints, a vertical process of regeneration within the existing built up areas offered the most viable way to accommodate future growth. This process of physical regeneration began with the gradual replacement of prestige frontages along the Lawnmarket and High Street by taller structures built in the tenement form. Eventually, the backlands and wynds (lanes) to the rear of the main facades were also redeveloped more intensively.

As the local economy of Edinburgh prospered, the standards of materials and construction were raised partly to reduce the risk of fires. Stone replaced timber as the preferred building material along the main street frontages. A technical innovation, in the form of the turnpike staircase, also facilitated the construction of taller buildings.[8] It is interesting to note that the most desirable multi-storey tenements usually contained accommodation for a range of income groups. Wealthier residents tended to live on the upper levels of the tenement, in spacious flats that provided a suite of rooms for different domestic functions, each with its own fireplace.[9]

The official boundaries of the Royal Burgh of Edinburgh remained virtually unchanged from 1300 until the Union of the Parliaments in 1707. Over this extensive period, the resident population increased by a factor of ten, to a level approaching 30,000.[10] By the beginning of the 18th century, Edinburgh was generally regarded as the capital of Scotland, and its role as a centre of government, religion, education and commerce was clearly established. Within the confines of the Royal Burgh, rich and poor sections of the population still lived in close proximity and had daily interaction that promoted a strong sense of mutual inter-dependence.

Once the pattern of vertical living had been firmly established in Edinburgh, tenement building spread to other Scottish burghs where the opportunities for outward growth were much less constrained. In these locations, the competition for commercial advantage was also generating pressures for redevelopment along the main thoroughfares, but the incentives for higher density forms of residential accommoda-

8. Robinson, 'Tenements: a pre-industrial tradition', p. 58.
9. Ibid., p. 63.
10. Ibid., p. 61.

tion were clearly less compelling than in Edinburgh. Wealthier merchants in the other burghs were generally in a more favourable position to build single-family town houses if they so desired. Why this practice was not more common in other Scottish burghs is uncertain, however, the subsequent experience of Georgian town extension schemes suggests that many affluent Scots were willing to occupy well-appointed tenement flats.

GEORGIAN TOWN EXTENSION SCHEMES

Political and economic conditions in Scotland changed significantly during the course of the 18th century. After the Union of the Parliaments in 1707, there was a marked increase in the volume of trade using Atlantic routes.[11] By the end of the 18th century, new forms of economic growth were clearly being generated by industrial innovations based on the application of steam power, the adoption of factory methods, and competitive advantages in the production of coal and iron ore.[12] With this improvement in economic performance, a portion of the newly created wealth was invested in planned 'town extension schemes' between 1750 and 1830. A key aim of town extension schemes was to offer more desirable housing options for the prospering middle classes. In the process, new developments were built on the periphery of larger cities and towns, well removed from the squalor and congestion of older medieval quarters.

In Scotland, the Georgian town extension schemes tended to provide a distinctive mix of purpose-built tenements and terraced houses. Edinburgh's New Town is the best known Scottish example of this form of provision, however, other noteworthy developments were undertaken in Glasgow, Dundee, Aberdeen, Greenock and Perth.[13] Along with various buildings of architectural merit, the town extension schemes of this period began to alter the physical and social structure of Scottish cities. These ventures applied innovative principles of site design on open land and established a new pattern of residential segregation along income lines.[14] By the middle of the 19th century, much clearer lines were drawn between middle class and working class neighbourhoods, and the deteriorating housing stock within the oldest parts of cities had

11. Richard Rodger, 'Building development' in M. Glendinning and D. Watters (eds.), *Home Builders – MacTaggart & Mickel and the Scottish Housebuilding Industry* (Edinburgh, 1999), Chapter B1, p. 193.
12. Ibid.
13. Peter J. Robinson, 'Tenements: the industrial legacy', *ROSC Review of Scottish Culture*, No. 2, 1986, p. 71.
14. Walker, 'The Glasgow grid', pp. 156-7.

been generally occupied by the poorest sections of the population.[15]

As a rule, Georgian town extension schemes in Scotland were laid out on a grid system that was intended to promote efficient circulation and to maximise the number of sites with a street frontage. A grid system of reasonable proportions also provided a framework for the construction of tenements in the form of 'hollow squares'. This pattern of tenement building became firmly established in Scotland during the Victorian period.

By 1840, the income levels of artisans, clerks, small shopkeepers and skilled industrial workers in Scotland had increased sufficiently to enable a market to emerge for modest forms of newly constructed tenement flats. This type of provision tended to be built on outlying sites in the vicinity of new industrial premises and associated railway lines.[16] Poorer sections of the population, including unskilled workers and casual labourers, had virtually no hope of affording the rent required for a newly built property, however modest. For these households, a move to marginally better accommodation within the older residential stock remained the only way of improving their housing circumstances.

15. Rodger, 'Building development', p. 196.
16. Ibid.
17. Ibid., p. 193.
18. Ibid.
19. Richard Rodger, 'The Victorian building industry and the housing of the Scottish working class' in M. Doughty (ed.), *Building the Industrial City* (Leicester, 1986), p. 185.

UNPRECEDENTED URBAN GROWTH

As industrial activities expanded, Scotland's urban population began to increase at an unprecedented rate. In 1800, only one-fifth of the total population lived in towns with 5,000 or more inhabitants. By 1861 this figure had doubled to two-fifths and by 1901 the proportion had reached nearly three-fifths.[17] This influx of people in search of work within the major cities placed enormous pressures on the availability of housing and the provision of local services. Over the course of the 19th century, Glasgow experienced a tenfold increase in population, Dundee and Aberdeen experienced a fivefold increase, and Edinburgh experienced a fourfold increase.[18]

The pressures of urban migration were especially acute between 1820 and 1860, when the regulations on building activities were generally ineffective.[19] Although various attempts were made to improve the control of building standards in urban areas through the passage of local acts, the situation remained highly problematic. The Burgh Police (Scotland) Act of 1862 also made little impact in part because the provisions were adoptive rather than mandatory.[20] Living conditions in the older town centres worsened dramatically in the face of cholera epidemics that transpired in 1832, 1848–49, and 1853–54.[21] The serious risks to public health were extensively documented in Edwin Chadwick's 1842 *Report on the Sanitary Condition of the Labouring Population of Great Britain*. In conducting this landmark study, Chadwick travelled to Scotland with Dr. Neil Arnott to inspect at first hand the situations within the most impoverished areas of Edinburgh and Glasgow. Their findings indicated that conditions in the wynds of Edinburgh's Old Town were the worst in Britain and conditions nearby Glasgow's Cathedral were only marginally better.[22]

DOMINANCE OF VICTORIAN TENEMENTS

Towards the end of the 19th century, stone-built tenements could be found in numerous locations across Scotland. The widespread diffusion of tenement living has been described by Colin McWilliam in the following terms:

> For those who needed housing and could afford to buy or rent it in new buildings, from skilled artisans to clerk and lower salaried professional man, the choice lay between the different areas of tenement development on the edge of every town. These were built throughout the last forty years of the century (with hardly a break in the depression of the 1870s which slowed down so many other kinds of investment), and wherever land values were high and sites were scarce, the tenement was universal. By 1900 few towns, even the smallest, were without their quota of at least one large, metropolitan looking flatted block; some of the latest examples, built in 1897, are called 'Jubilee Buildings'. More typically, built up along indefinite lengths of street on the edges of larger places, they provide the most characteristic experience of Victorian townscape.[23]

During the Victorian era skilled workers in English cities were usually able to occupy modest single-family terraced houses with private

20. Rodger, 'Building development', p. 193.
21. Ibid., p. 194.
22. Ibid., p. 195.
23. Colin McWilliam, *Scottish Townscape* (London, 1975), p. 151.

gardens. As economic conditions improved, the market provision of new artisan housing shifted from back-to-back properties to 'through' terraced houses. In contrast, as the Scottish economy developed during this period, the general standard of working class tenements was raised through the reform of building regulations but there were relatively few attempts to provide lower density accommodation for artisans in urban locations on a purely commercial basis.

Richard Rodger has examined the underlying reasons for this variation in the forms of new artisan housing. His findings point to the following combination of economic factors:

> It was the relative strength of consumer demand and the responsiveness of supply which accounted more precisely for the distinctive housing in England and Scotland. Of crucial importance were the relative levels of disposable incomes as an indicator of the strength of effective demand, and the availability and price of building land and the costs of construction as major constituents of supply response.[24]

In the Scottish case, several factors on the supply side of the market raised the costs of new development. Building materials tended to be more expensive than in England. The Scottish system of land tenure known as feuing, and more particularly the heritable securities that could be raised on security of future feu duties, served to inflate land values in the larger cities and towns. On the demand side, the potential for the development of new artisan housing was generally constrained by lower wage levels and rigidities in the rental housing market. According to Rodger, trade-specific comparisons of average wage levels indicated that workers in Scotland were paid 20 to 30 per cent less than workers in England, whereas the level of rents charged for housing in Scotland were higher than the rent levels found in any of the English regions apart from London.[25]

Conditions in Scotland were also influenced by an inflexible system of yearly lettings. Working class households in England benefited from the availability of relatively short tenancies, which enabled them to react fairly quickly to sharp reductions in income. By comparison, in order to gain access to a given property in Scotland, tenants with meagre resources were generally required to make a 1-year commitment for

24. Rodger, 'The invisible hand – market forces, housing and the urban form in Victorian cities', p. 195.
25. Ibid.

the payment of rent. For the poorest sections of the population, the choice of housing was essentially driven by a need to reduce the risk of eviction. Given the high rent levels found in Scottish cities, the housing in working class areas was commonly seen to offer poor value for money. As a consequence, many households on low incomes opted for a very basic standard of accommodation and were reluctant to spend more on rent in order to improve their housing circumstances.

MOUNTING THREATS TO PUBLIC HEALTH

By the mid-1860s, living conditions within British cities had deteriorated to the point where new forms of intervention were seen to be warranted on public health grounds. Initially a small number of local authorities sought parliamentary approval for private legislation that was intended to promote more effective remedial measures. Among the key innovations were new powers to implement area-based sanitary improvement schemes. These schemes were designed to remove or upgrade larger concentrations of substandard properties, in order to make a greater impact on living conditions than was possible by improving individual dwellings.

26. Rodger, 'The Victorian building industry and the housing of the Scottish working class', p. 183.

Parliamentary approval for this type of private legislation was obtained by Liverpool Town Council in 1864, Glasgow Town Council in 1866, and Edinburgh Town Council in 1867. Over the next two decades, more general provisions for area-based sanitary improvement schemes were included in a series of enabling statutes known as the Cross Acts. Under this legislation, local authorities were permitted but not required to carry out schemes of this type. The available powers were used sparingly in English cities. The response in Scotland was somewhat more pro-active, perhaps because an area-based approach was more essential to make an impact on tenement conditions. The earlier area-based sanitary improvement schemes in Glasgow and Edinburgh were followed by similar initiatives approved for parts of Dundee in 1871, Greenock in 1877, Leith in 1877 and Aberdeen in 1882.[26]

The responses in Scotland usually involved the demolition of sizeable areas of derelict property and the promotion of a comprehensive approach to the redevelopment of large clearance sites. Relatively little attention was given to the possibilities for upgrading existing buildings. These early slum clearance initiatives proved to be highly contentious. Although a substantial amount of poor quality housing was demolished in central locations, little effort was made to ensure that the displaced local residents were adequately rehoused. The associated improvements in public health were fairly negligible since the underlying problems of destitution and overcrowding were simply shifted to adjacent areas of run down housing. Local rate-payers were often less than enthusiastic to cover the substantial losses that were usually incurred in the implementation of slum clearance schemes. At this stage, central government was only interested in promoting remedial action on the part of local authorities, and there were no provisions for any financial assistance to offset operating losses.

Medical Officers of Health played a key role in designating the 'unhealthy areas' that were the subject of area-based sanitary improvement schemes. In some instances, pioneering empirical studies were undertaken to provide the basis for these decisions. These investigations attempted to clarify the spatial distribution of mortality and morbidity rates within the given city. In Edinburgh, Dr. Henry Littlejohn produced a landmark report in 1865, which broke new ground in documenting the state of living conditions within the most disadvantaged parts of Scotland's capital city.

Dr. James Burn Russell, who served as Glasgow's Medical Officer of Health from 1872 to 1898, was an outspoken critic of the tenement system. He was particularly concerned about the harmful effects of 3 interrelated forms of crowding: (1) over-building of sites which resulted in an excessive numbers of tenements on a given parcel of land, (2) over-provision of dwellings within a given tenement which resulted in excessive numbers of flats with basic design faults and (3) over-crowding of persons within the dwelling which resulted in a serious imbalance between the number of occupants and the amount of available internal space.[27] In his writings, Dr. Russell argued that these forms of crowding were 'generally found together, each intensifying the evil effects of the other, and all together producing that state of chronic ill-health, with acute exacerbations, which is a feature of the life of Glasgow'.[28] He was also critical of the conventional arrangement of Victorian tenements in 'hollow squares' which inhibited the free circulation of air, and was keen to eliminate any additional buildings within the enclosed space.[29]

The problem of severe over-crowding within the home was much

27. James Burn Russell, 'On the Immediate results of the operations of the Glasgow Improvement Trust at May, 1874' in A. K. Chalmers (ed.), *Public Health Administration in Glasgow* (Glasgow, 1905), p. 102.
28. Ibid.
29. Ibid., p. 103.

36

more pervasive in Scotland than in England – particularly so in the West of Scotland. According to the 1901 Census, as much as one-sixth of the population of the Burgh of Glasgow were living in 1-room dwellings.[30] The day-to-day experience of tenement living had a strong influence on the development of local culture. In addition to engendering a spirit of mutual support, the pressures created by the lack of internal space and the over-development of sites had numerous repercussions for the general pattern of everyday life. As Richard Rodger has observed,

> Privacy was virtually an impossibility, and the behavioural stand-ards of morality and propriety associated with separate sleeping arrangements for boys and girls, for parents and children, and for family members and lodgers, were difficult to achieve. Per-sonal hygiene, sexual relations and family life were conducted in an atmosphere of communality. This was reinforced by the collective amenities of tenement houses – sanitary provisions, running water, and washing facilities were normally shared be-tween several families. In contrast to the more self-contained space and privacy of the terraced house, Scottish tenement life was governed by confined, shared spaces, and this affected youth culture and patterns of child-care, just as it did games and gossip.[31]

30. Cd. 4016, Return shewing the Housing Conditions of the Population of Scotland, 1908, Table II, p. 4.
31. Rodger, 'Building development', p. 203.

DECK ACCESS BLOCKS AND COTTAGE FLATS

Between 1840 and 1900, within urban parts of Scotland, conventional tenements accounted for the vast proportion of newly built working class dwellings. These properties were normally developed on a purely commercial basis. In the prevailing economic conditions, tenements were generally considered to be the only commercially viable form of new construction for working class households. Any departures from the conventional pattern of tenement building were usually under-taken by philanthropic bodies or progressive local authorities that wished to demonstrate how some of the more obvious disadvantages of tenement living could be eliminated.

These attempts to find viable alternatives to the conventional pat-tern of tenement provision generally involved two types of innovation in the design of working class dwellings. One approach was to build multi-storey blocks of walk-up flats with deck access to the properties above ground level. In the Scottish context, this innovation can be seen as an effort to reform the tenement tradition along lines favoured by the public health movement. The second innovation was to build a lower density, hybrid form of accommodation that has become known as 'cottage flats'. This form of provision attempted to incorporate some of the desirable features of English-style terraced housing, such as individual entrance doors and private gardens, within a 2-storey flatted format. The earliest examples of cottage flats were built in terraces, but the basic concept was later adapted as free-standing blocks of 4 flats, each provided with an entrance door and a private garden at ground level.

The first deck access blocks in Scotland were built during the 1850s. These developments were influenced by the architectural projects of Henry Roberts, undertaken in London on behalf of the Society for Improving the Conditions of the Labouring Classes. Roberts was responsible for designing a flatted development in Bloomsbury's Streatham Street, known as the 'Model Houses for Families'. In many respects, the design of this 4-storey structure was an architectural response to the cholera epidemics of the 1840s. It consisted entirely of self-contained flats arranged round a U-shaped internal court, with gallery access for the units above ground level.[32] When the development was officially

32. John Nelson Tarn, *Five Per Cent Philanthropy* (Cambridge, 1973), pp. 18-20.

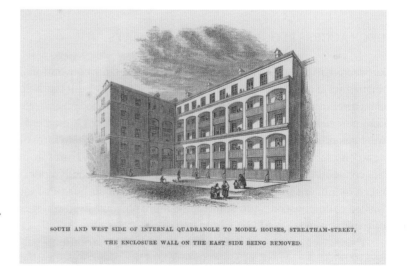

RIGHT: Inner Courtyard of Model Houses for Families, Bloomsbury, designed by Henry Roberts for the Society for Improving the Conditions of the Labouring Classes.

SOUTH AND WEST SIDE OF INTERNAL QUADRANGLE TO MODEL HOUSES, STREATHAM-STREET, THE ENCLOSURE WALL ON THE EAST SIDE BEING REMOVED.

THE MODEL HOUSES FOR FAMILIES, IN STREATHAM-STREET, BLOOMSBURY.

LEFT: Frontage of Model Houses for Families, Bloomsbury.

33. Ibid.
34. Jim Johnson and Lou Rosenburg, *Renewing Old Edinburgh – The Enduring Legacy of Patrick Geddes* (Glendaruel, 2010), pp. 102-7.

opened in the spring of 1850, it was widely praised in the press as a healthy living environment for the future residents.[33]

From a public health standpoint, deck access blocks offered a number of potential advantages over conventional Scottish tenements. Sanitary reformers of the period were concerned to ensure that all living spaces had proper ventilation and adequate daylight. The provision of deck access for flats on the upper levels of the building had two major advantages in public health terms. It facilitated 'through and through' ventilation within each dwelling and significantly reduced the amount of enclosed common space which tended to trap foul air.

A number of Victorian deck access blocks have survived in Edinburgh. The earliest examples, dating from the mid-1850s, were Rosemount Buildings in Gardner's Crescent and Patriothall in the Stockbridge area. Both were sponsored by semi-philanthropic bodies that aimed to promote healthful model dwellings in a flatted form. Towards the end of the 19th century, the local authority built 3 deck access blocks on slum clearance sites in the heart of the Old Town. These developments were completed at High School Yards in 1897, Tron Square in 1900, and Portsburgh Square in 1901.[34]

The origins of cottage flats are more difficult to pin down. Under the

ABOVE: Rosemount Buildings,
deck access housing in Gardner's
Crescent, Fountainbridge,
Edinburgh. (Photo: John Reiach)

RIGHT: Stockbridge 'Colonies',
Edinburgh. (Photo: John Reiach)

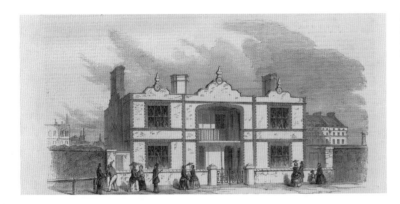

LEFT: The Prince Consort's Modern Cottages designed by Henry Roberts for the Great Exhibition, London, 1851.

patronage of HRH Prince Albert, Henry Roberts also designed a proto-type for working class families that formed part of the Great Exhibition of 1851. This 2-storey structure, known as the Prince Consort's Model Cottages, was constructed within the grounds of the Cavalry Barracks in Hyde Park.[35] The term 'model cottages' was somewhat misleading since the structure consisting of 4 self-contained flats was intended to be built in 2-storey terraces.[36]

Another possible precedent was the Tyneside flat, a vernacular form of housing found mainly in Newcastle, Gateshead and South Shields.[37] Like the conventional Scottish tenements, Tyneside flats were a com-mercial response to specific economic and geographic conditions. These properties were constructed of brick in 2-storey terraces, with the space under one roof divided horizontally to provide a lower and an upper flat, each with separate entrances at the front and back.[38] This form of working class housing was widely built on Tyneside from the 1860s. The 1911 Census indicated that over three-fifths of all households within the Tyneside area were flat-dwellers.[39]

Other potential precedents for cottage flats may be found within Scottish locations. As noted previously, 2-storey structures were often built in fishing and weaving villages with workspace space on one level and living accommodation on the other. This form of vernacular build-ing may well have been adapted for the provision of 2-storey cottage flats.[40] Edinburgh has a particularly rich legacy of cottage flats, which is largely due to the enduring popularity of 'Colonies' developments sponsored by the Edinburgh Co-operative Building Company between 1861 and 1914.[41] Other interesting examples of cottage flats can be found

35. Tarn, *Five Percent Philanthropy*, pp. 20-1.
36. Ibid.
37. Rodger, *Housing in Urban Britain, 1780–1914*, (Cam-bridge, 1995), pp. 35-6.
38. M. J. Daunton, *House and Home in the Victorian City* (London, 1983), pp. 42-3.
39. Ibid. p. 40.
40. For example, see McWil-liam, *Scottish Townscape*, pp. 153-4.
41. See Richard Rodger, *Edin-burgh's Colonies* (Glendaruel, 2011).

RIGHT: Cottage flats in Deanston, near Stirling.

at Burntisland and Denbeath in Fife; Fisherrow, Musselburgh in East Lothian; Rutherglen and Scotstoun in Glasgow; Motherwell, Wishaw, and Bellshill in Lanarkshire; the Whitecrook district of Clydebank; Bannockburn and Deanston in Stirlingshire.

ARTISAN COTTAGES IN URBAN AREAS

Single-family artisan cottages are relatively uncommon in Scottish cities, due to the high costs of land and construction. The vast majority of Victorian and Edwardian terraced housing in Scotland was built for middle class families rather than better-off working class households. There are, however, some noteworthy Scottish examples of purpose-built artisan cottages in a number of urban locations. The earliest 19th century examples are similar to the single-storey terraced cottages frequently found in mining, fishing and farming villages.

At the mouth of Aberdeen's Harbour, the community of Footdee (aka Fittie) was originally built in 1809 as a planned development to rehouse the families of local fishermen. This area was originally laid out in two squares by John Smith, the Superintendent of Public Works. Later developments of artisan cottages can be found in Edinburgh (within the Wester Coates area near Haymarket and the Lorne area of Leith), in Glasgow (within

ABOVE: Artisan cottages in Fittee, Aberdeen. (Photo: C. Bremner)

LEFT: Artisan cottages in Wester Coates, Edinburgh. (Photo: J. Rosser)

RIGHT: Artisan cottage housing in Dumbarton Road, Scotstoun, Glasgow.

Dumbarton Rd, Scotstoun.

42. Derived from information presented in the Burgh of Glasgow Valuation Roll, FY 1914/15.

Whiteinch, Scotstoun, Jordanhill and Claythorn), in Falkirk (Philips and Gibsongray Streets), and in Dumbarton (Knoxland Square and Wallace Street). The developments of this type in Falkirk and Dumbarton were sponsored by mutual aid building societies interested in promoting working class owner-occupation.

The Glasgow developments at Whiteinch and Scotstoun were closely linked to the growth of shipbuilding on the Clyde from the 1860s. These areas to the west of the city centre contain the largest concentration of artisan cottages in a major Scottish city. The bulk of this housing was built between 1895 and 1914 by the Scotstoun Estates Building Company, set up by the local landowner. Within the Scotstoun area, the Company provided more than 600 single- and 2-storey cottages of stone construction. The initial residents were a mix of skilled industrial workers, small proprietors and lower-paid white collar employees, a majority of whom were able to take advantage of a house purchase scheme offered by the developer.[42]

Scotstoun's artisan cottages have remained highly popular and well cared for by the local residents. A Conservation Area was declared by the local authority in 1987. Although sometimes described as a development inspired by garden city principles, the first phase of construction was undertaken 3 years before the publication of Ebenezer Howard's book. Neither the rectilinear street pattern nor the design features of the terraced houses are typical of the 'open style' of development favoured by the garden city movement. In terms of built form, the more likely influences were some of the model industrial villages sponsored by progressive employers in various part of England.

MAJOR DECLINE IN TENEMENT CONSTRUCTION

Along with a number of other European countries, Britain experienced a long-term decline in housebuilding which began in the 1870s and continued until the end of WW1. This downward trend was initially triggered by a general trade depression in the early 1870s.[43] The situation in Scotland was exacerbated by the crash of the City of Glasgow Bank in 1878. Within the housing sector of the economy, the repercussions were particularly evident at the cheaper end of the new build market. As the volume of working class tenement construction declined, questions were increasingly raised about the continuing viability of commercial development for this type of accommodation.

Although the volume of housebuilding in Scotland improved some-what during the 1890s, it fell back to the point where the construction of working class tenements came to a virtual standstill around 1905.[44] A number of factors contributed to this acute decline, which occurred at a time when wage differentials between Scotland and England were narrowing in real terms.[45] Within Scotland, any increases in real wages were more than offset by the rising costs of tenement construction during this period, largely driven by the adoption of higher minimum standards under local building regulations. Faced with diminishing profit margins, many private investors that had been providing resources for the construction of working class tenements now turned to government gilts for a safer and more favourable return.[46]

According to Richard Rodger, a number of Scottish builders had expanded their operations significantly by the close of the 19th century, yet this increase in scale did not prevent the sharp decline at the cheaper end of the new build market.[47] Private builders often assumed that local authorities would eventually step in to meet the need for this type of residential construction. Between 1890 and 1914, Scottish local authorities used the provisions of the 1890 Housing of the Working Classes Act to build approximately 3,500 dwellings mainly in the form of traditional tenements or deck access blocks in urban locations.

43. Rodger, *Housing in Urban Britain, 1780-1914*, p. 52.
44. Rodger, 'The Victorian building industry and the housing of the Scottish working class', p. 188.
45. Ibid., p. 182.
46. Ibid., p. 197.
47. Ibid., p. 181.

In those parts of Scotland where shipbuilding and heavy industries were expanding, the collapse of tenement building posed significant problems for employers that needed to recruit additional staff. A number of firms took measures to ensure that adequate housing was available for their incoming workers.[48] In some instances, accommodation was developed by the firm directly. These developments were primarily undertaken in order to meet the labour supply needs of the firm, and earning a normal commercial return on the housing was usually a secondary consideration. In other cases, private builders were commissioned to construct the necessary accommodation, often with some support from the firm with respect to the provision of land and working capital.

Over the course of the 19th century, there is little evidence of a sustained debate in Scotland either about the need to put an end to tenement construction or the need to provide cottage accommodation for working class families in urban areas. In Scottish reform circles, the debates about urban housing problems tended to focus on how best to improve the situations of the poorest households in the worst conditions, who had no hope of being able to afford the rent for newly built dwellings of any description.

A debate about the development of cottages versus tenements did, however, materialise in Scotland after the passage of the Housing and Town Planning Act of 1909. Among other things, this legislation provided new powers for the preparation of town planning schemes for undeveloped land on the periphery of larger cities and towns. Since the turn of the century, the garden city movement had been actively campaigning about the problems that were being generated by uncontrolled suburban sprawl. Initially, the garden city movement became better known in Scotland through the efforts to promote the preparation of town planning schemes. Before describing the influence of garden city ideas north of the Border, it is necessary to outline the broad pattern of development of the mainstream garden city movement from 1900 to 1939.

48. Rodger, *Housing in Urban Britain, 1780–1914*, p. 52.

2 Mainstream Garden City Movement 1900–1939

PREVIOUS PAGE: Sir Ebenezer
Howard, founder of the garden
city movement and author of
*Tomorrow: A Peaceful Path to Real
Reform*.

BELOW: Painting by Spencer Gore
titled 'Letchworth: The Road 1912'.
(Reproduced by kind permission
of North Hertfordshire Museums
Service)

This chapter traces the early development of the mainstream garden city movement from 1900 to 1939. The discussion is not intended as a comprehensive account of all of the various interests and activities of the movement. Particular attention is given to issues concerned with working class housing, which strongly influenced the specific course of events in Scotland.

When considering the origins of the garden city movement, Dennis Hardy has stressed the importance of taking into account the mounting pressures for social reform that were being generated by class tensions and the negative impacts of industrialisation and urbanisation.[1] At the close of the 19th century the British countryside was in a chronic state of depression. The sustained outflow of population from rural areas had produced major concentrations of poverty, unemployment and overcrowding within the larger cities and towns. To compound matters, the British economy was facing stiff competition from German and American business interests, which threatened the country's leading position in manufacturing and commerce. The growing tensions amongst the world's main trading nations produced an accelerating arms race which included a major commitment in Britain to naval rearmament.

In developing his basic ideas for garden cities, Ebenezer Howard (1850–1928) drew inspiration from various sources including the writings of James Silk Buckingham, Edward Bellamy, Henry George, John Ruskin and William Morris. On a more practical level, the appearance of impressive new industrial villages at Port Sunlight (dating from 1888) and Bournville (dating from 1893) raised awareness of the possibilities

1. Dennis Hardy, *From Garden Cities to New Towns: Campaigning for town and country planning, 1899–1946* (London, 1991), p. 2.

49

POETS' CORNER, PORT SUNLIGHT.

for combatting the problems associated with uncontrolled urban growth. These enlightened efforts by major employers were indicative of both the need and potential for a broader strategy to develop self-contained communities which were based on an 'open style' of physical planning and low density housing design. The residential areas of Port Sunlight and Bournville were intended to provide a varied range of cottage ac-

commodation for working class families, embracing an architectural style that was strongly influenced by the English arts and crafts movement. These areas generally featured imaginatively designed groups of individual dwellings, picturesque streetscapes which were well adapted to the natural setting, and generous amounts of open space and communal facilities for the benefit of the residents.

EBENEZER HOWARD'S VISION

The basic ideas for gardens cities were conceived by Ebenezer Howard as the key element within a broad strategy for social reform. This broad strategy was aimed at curbing excessive agglomeration within and around the major cities, promoting planned decentralisation of population and industry from the existing urban centres to new self-contained settlements, improving working class housing conditions, regenerating the rural economy, and protecting the countryside from the encroachment of uncontrolled urban sprawl. The proposed garden cities were conceived as a new type of living environment which would simultaneously incorporate the best features of urban and rural living and eliminate the worst ones. Howard outlined his general approach in a seminal book which was originally published in 1898 under the title *Tomorrow – a Peaceful Path to Real Reform* and reissued with minor modifications in 1902 as *Garden Cities of Tomorrow*.

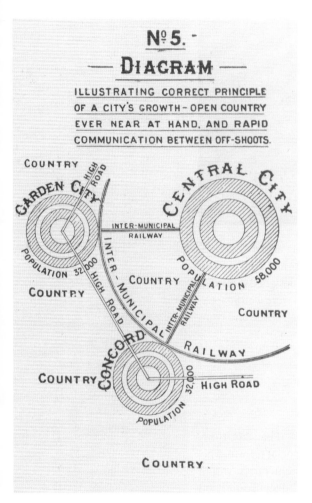

Nº 5.

— DIAGRAM —

ILLUSTRATING CORRECT PRINCIPLE
OF A CITY'S GROWTH – OPEN COUNTRY
EVER NEAR AT HAND, AND RAPID
COMMUNICATION BETWEEN OFF-SHOOTS.

ABOVE: Howard's diagram showing desired relationship between a new garden city and an existing central city.

2. Michael Hughes (ed.), *The Letters of Lewis Mumford and Frederic J. Osborn: A Transatlantic Dialogue 1938–70* (New York, 1972), p. 453.

Ebenezer Howard was a Londoner by birth, from a Non-Conformist family of modest means. Although often described as a utopian thinker, Howard was essentially a pragmatic idealist rather than a dreamer of unachievable radical schemes.[2] For most of his working life he earned a living as a court stenographer, yet managed to retain both his passion for inventing things and his general optimism about the potential benefits of scientific progress. He had little talent for politics, but was familiar with the key political issues of the day. His personal prescriptions for social reform were shaped by the writings of evolutionary socialists who favoured co-operation and decentralisation. Consequently, his garden city vision was strongly based on a voluntary approach that was thought to be achievable without a fundamental restructuring of British society.

Howard's notion of combining the best features of town and country living was communicated effectively in his famous diagram called 'The Three Magnets'. As envisaged in his book, the physical development of a proper garden city would require the acquisition of 6,000 acres of farmland at a valuation based on agricultural use. On 1,000 acres of the site, a new self-contained settlement was to be built with living accommodation and employment opportunities for 30,000 residents. The remaining 5,000 acres would form a greenbelt that was to be reserved mainly for open space and agricultural uses capable of supporting another 2,000 persons in rural occupations. Once the target population of 32,000 had been reached, no further expansion of the given garden city was to be permitted. Any pressures for additional growth within the general area were to be met through the creation of a planned network of similar settlements beyond the agricultural belt.

Howard made no claims to be a trained designer. His book included a schematic diagram for the layout of a garden city based on a circular

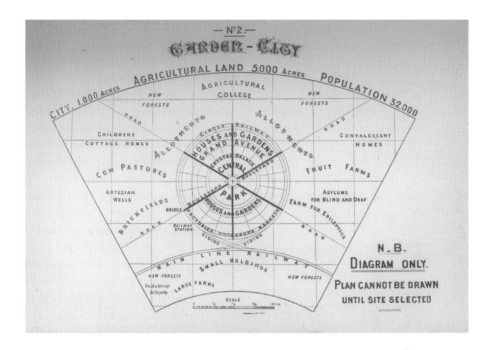

— No 2.—

GARDEN - CITY

AGRICULTURAL LAND 5.000 ACRES   POPULATION 32,000

CITY. 1.000 ACRES

AGRICULTURAL
COLLEGE

NEW
FORESTS

NEW
FORESTS

ROAD

CHILDRENS
COTTAGE HOMES

ALLOTMENTS

CIRCLE   RAILWAY

HOUSES AND GARDENS
GRAND AVENUE

CRISTAL PALACE

CENTRAL

ALLOTMENTS

ROAD

CONVALESCENT
HOMES

COW PASTURES

PARK

FRUIT   FARMS

ARTESIAN
WELLS

BRICKFIELDS

BRIDGE

BOULEVARD

HOUSES AND GARDENS

BOULEVARD

FACTORIES WORKSHOPS MARKETS

FARM FOR EPILEPTICS

FARM

ASYLUMS
FOR BLIND AND DEAF

RAILWAY
STATION

SIDING

SIDING

ROAD

MAIN   LINE   RAILWAY

SMALL HOLDINGS

NEW FORESTS

NEW FORESTS

Industrial
Schools

LARGE FARMS

SCALE

MILE

N . B.

DIAGRAM ONLY.

PLAN CANNOT BE DRAWN
UNTIL SITE SELECTED

geometric form. This diagram, he later confessed, was not meant as a precise blueprint for the physical development of a garden city. Through his efforts to establish the first garden city at Letchworth, he came to recognise that the preferred site plan for a garden city should be adapted to the local topography and available communication links, rather than be based on any preconceived geometric solution.

A good deal of attention was given in his book to questions concerning the administrative and financial arrangements for the development of a garden city. As a firm believer in the benefits of voluntary co-operation, he was generally optimistic about the prospects for creating the desired self-contained settlements without any form of financial assistance from the state. Any necessary capital would be raised by a private trust offering a limited but reasonable return to potential investors, and the entire site would be held in common ownership so that any future increases in land value could be leveraged to provide long-term benefits for the whole community.

ABOVE: Howard's schematic plan for a new garden city, with caveat stating it is essential to adapt the layout for any actual development to the relevant site conditions.

FOUNDING OF THE GARDEN CITY ASSOCIATION

Shortly after the publication of *Tomorrow – A Peaceful Path to Real Reform*, the Garden City Association was formed in London to promote Howard's ideas. This body was established in 1899, and has remained in existence to the present day, albeit the name of the organisation has been changed on two occasions. When the Housing and Town Planning Act of 1909 was about to receive parliamentary approval, the name of the Garden City Association was changed to the Garden Cities and Town Planning Association. More than 3 decades later, in 1941, it was changed again to the Town and Country Planning Association in order to recognise the vital contributions that were being made within rural areas during World War Two (WW2).

At the outset, the members of the Garden City Association were mainly a small band of activists with interests in radical causes such as land reform.[3] After a few months in operation, however, Howard was in a position to report on the growth and diversification of the membership in the following terms:

The Association numbers amongst its members, Manufacturers, Co-operators, Architects, Artists, Medical Men, Financial Experts, Lawyers, Merchants, Ministers of Religion, Members of the L.C.C. (Moderate and Progressive), Socialists and Individuals, Radicals and Conservatives.[4]

BELOW: Listing of office bearers of the Garden City Association, 1906.

3. Hardy, *From Garden Cities to New Towns*, p. 16.
4. Ebenezer Howard, *Garden Cities of Tomorrow* (London, 1902), p. 165. This statement originally appeared in the publication *Citizen*.

Garden City Association.

MEMBERS OF COUNCIL (April 4th, 1906).

Chairman : MR. JUSTICE NEVILLE.

*Thomas Adams.   *A. H. H. Matthews.
Percy Alden M.P.   *Budgett Meakin.
Mrs. Barnett.   Rev. C. Moor.
*Rev. J. B. Booth, M.A.   *R. O. Moon, M.D., M.R.C.P.
Col. F. S. Bowring, C.B., R.E.   *Edward R. P. Moon.
George Crosbie.   *Miss M. E. Nicholson.
*Warwick H. Draper, M.A.   Rev. A. W. Oxford.
F. W. Flear.   Dr. Paton.
Hon. Dudley F. Fortescue.   *Mrs. H. D. Pearsall.
*Miss G. M. Gibson.   Rev. Canon Rawnsley.
*Miss Sybella Gurney.   George Rose (Liverpool).
*G. Montagu Harris, M.A.   Hon. R. Russell, M.A., F.R.M.S.
Walter Hazell.   W. H. Gurney Salter.
Lady Helmsley.   *Edward T. Sturdy.
Ebenezer Howard.   Alderman Thompson
T. M. Kirkwood.   *Herbert Warren, B.A.
*H. C. Lander, A.R.I.B.A.   Aneurin Williams, M.A.
Frederick Litchfield.

*Members of Executive.

OFFICERS.

Chairman of Executive : Dr. R. O. Moon.
Hon. Treasurer : Dr. Arthur James.
Secretary : Ewart G. Culpin, 602-3, High Holborn, W.C.
Hon. Sec. of East of Scotland : G. F. Henderson, W.S., 23, Rutland Square, Edinburgh.
Hon. Sec. of West of Scotland : Laurence R. Brown, 216, West George Street, Glasgow.
Hon. Sec. of Manchester District : T. W. Greenwood, 44, Brazenose Street.
     ,,   Liverpool District : T. Alwyn Lloyd, 20, Grove Park.
     ,,   Leicester : N. P. Laird, Thurnby, near Leicester.

Branches are being formed in other parts of the Country.

Conveners of Sectional Committees.

(1) *Prospecting and Development* : Herbert Warren, B.A.
(2) *Legal, Parliamentary and Local Government* : Warwick H. Draper, M.A.
(3) *Housing and Public Health* : Dr. R. O. Moon.
(4) *Architecture and Building* : H. Clapham Lander, A.R.I.B.A.
(5) *Agriculture, Allotments and Small Holdings* : A. H. H. Matthews.
(6) *Engineering, Roads, etc.* : Colonel Bowring, C.B., R.E.

Foreign Correspondents and Hon. Secretaries.

Paris : Georges Benoit-Levy, 97, Quai d'Orsey, Paris. (*Tel.* 524-07.)
Berlin : Bernard Kampffmeyer, Garzau, bei Rohrfelde, Ostbahn.
Brussels : Charles Didier, 33, Rue Forestiere, Brussels.
The Hague : J. L. Bruyn, Kepplerstraat, 170, The Hague, Holland.

LEFT: Ebenezer Howard
delivering speech at a Letchworth
Conference.

5. Hardy, *From Garden Cities to New Towns*, p. 46.
6. Michael Simpson, *Thomas Adams and the Modern Planning Movement* (London, 1985), p. 12.

By the start of 1901, the body of members included as many as 350 persons, and an office had been opened in central London which was staffed by a full-time paid secretary.[5] Sir Ralph Neville (1848–1918), a prominent Liberal with numerous contacts in the business community had agreed to serve as Chairman of the Garden City Association. Thomas Adams (1870–1940), an energetic young Scot from the village of Corstorphine near Edinburgh had been employed as Secretary on a full-time basis. Adams combined his farming background with a genuine talent for journalism and a keen interest in the Land Question. After only 3 months in post, he was able to organise a well attended conference to promote the garden city cause.

This conference was held during September 1901 at Bournville, the model industrial village that had recently been promoted by George Cadbury. The gathering afforded an opportunity to observe at first hand the results of the Cadbury initiative and to consider the implications for the future development of garden cities.[6] More than 300 delegates attended the event, including a number of MPs and representatives from municipalities, professional organisations, churches, trade unions, reform groups and co-operative societies. One of the keynote speakers was Raymond Unwin, an architect-planner who was soon to become a leading figure in the garden city movement. The discussions, which focused on issues relating to town planning, housing reform and the construction of self-contained garden cities, were widely reported in the press.

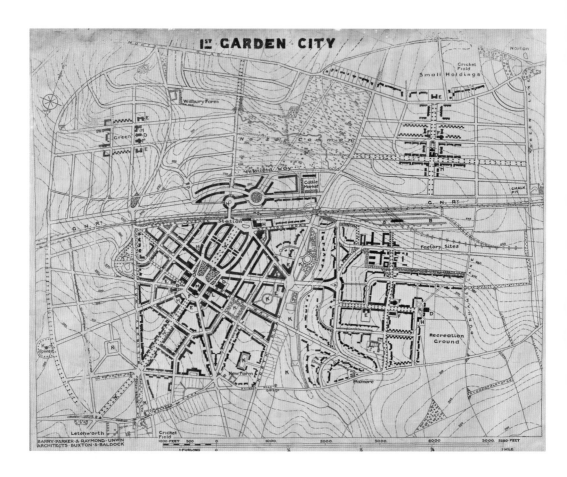

ABOVE: Initial plan for Letchworth, prepared by Parker and Unwin for *First Garden City Limited*. (Garden City Collection, Letchworth Garden City Heritage Foundation)

7. Hardy, *From Garden Cities to New Towns*, p. 47.

LAUNCH OF LETCHWORTH

Howard had a strong desire to link theory and practice. He realised it would be difficult to promote a broad strategy for the development of garden cities without an actual example. During the formative years of the Garden City Association, the primary objective was to create the first garden city. With this in mind, the Garden City Pioneer Company was set up in July 1902, with a share capital of £20,000.[7] The main

Duke of Devonshire opening Cheap Cottages
Exhibition, Letchworth.
(GARDEN CITY SERIES.)

LEFT: Official opening of the
Cheap Cottages Exhibition at
Letchworth, by the Duke of
Devonshire.

BELOW: Letchworth promotional
poster. (Garden City Collection,
Letchworth Garden City Heritage
Foundation)

8. Ibid.
9. Mervyn Miller, *English Garden Cities* (Swindon, 2010),
p. 18.

functions of this body were concerned with finding a suitable site for
the first garden city comprising a sufficient amount of available agricultural land, and raising the necessary funds for its acquisition. By
the close of 1902 the fundraising target of £20,000 had been achieved,
in part through generous subscriptions from influential garden city
supporters such as Alfred Harmsworth and W. H. Lever.[8]

A wide-ranging search eventually yielded a suitable site in Hertfordshire about 40 miles from central London on the Great Northern
Railway. This site at Letchworth consisted of 6 square miles of rolling
countryside. Once the land had been acquired, the Pioneer Company
was wound up and a new body named First Garden City Ltd was formed
to take the project forward. At this stage a limited competition was organised to explore possibilities for the overall layout of the site. Three
design teams were invited to make submissions – William Lethaby and
Halsay Riccardo; Geoffry Lucas and Sidney Cranfield; and Barry Parker
and Raymond Unwin.[9] In February 1904, the Board of Directors of First
Garden City Ltd officially endorsed the Parker and Unwin submission,
which was seen to be a sensitive application of Howard's ideas to the
physical features of the site. By the end of 1904, the construction phase
had begun in earnest.

Various problems were encountered in the course of implementation.
It proved difficult to obtain the necessary loan finance for the provision
of infrastructure and to attract the desired mix of industries for the

HEALTH of the COUNTRY
COMFORTS of the TOWN

LETCHWORTH
The FIRST GARDEN CITY

10. Ibid., p. 22.

11. Ibid.

12. Mark Swenarton, *Artisans and Architects* (Basingstoke and London, 1989), p. 127.

13. Mervyn Miller, 'Raymond Unwin 1863–1940' in Gordon E. Cherry (ed.), *Pioneers in British Planning* (London, 1981), p. 73.

14. Ibid., pp. 74-5.

15. Ibid., p. 75.

16. Ibid., p. 78.

17. Ibid.

manufacturing base of the garden city.[10] Questions about how best to provide a distinctive civic core for the new settlement were not easy to resolve. Nevertheless, the emerging form of Letchworth was generally regarded as an imaginative attempt to integrate town and country, as well as a useful demonstration of the functional principles of land-use planning. An impressive range of low density housing was provided for skilled working class and middle class residents, along with a generous allocation of land for open space and recreational uses.[11]

Many visitors came to Letchworth to observe the rate of progress, from other parts of Britain and abroad. Often the delegations from the Continent were from countries which, like Scotland, had a long tradition of tenement living. These visitors were particularly impressed by the cottage accommodation provided within the artisan quarters of the garden city. The attractive character of these areas was in many respects due to the sensitive design ideas of Raymond Unwin and the collective principles of housing co-partnership promoted by Henry Vivian.

CONTRIBUTION OF RAYMOND UNWIN

Raymond Unwin (1863–1940) firmly believed that architecture and town planning could make a vital contribution towards improving the living conditions of ordinary people.[12] Over the course of a long and varied career, he never lost sight of the importance of ensuring that all sections of society had decent places to live and work.

Unwin was born in Derbyshire and spent his formative years living in Oxford with his family. In the early 1880s he returned north to take up an engineering apprenticeship at Chesterfield.[13] Subsequently, during 1887, he was employed as an engineer by the Staveley Iron and Coal Company in Derbyshire. This post enabled him to gain valuable experience in site layout and the design of housing for industrial workers.[14] Nearly a decade later he entered into partnership with his brother-in-law Barry Parker, who was a qualified architect.[15] Their practice, known as Parker and Unwin, was initially involved mainly in the design of individual houses for relatively affluent middle class families. Once the garden city movement had emerged, the firm was presented with a range of new opportunities to focus upon innovative types of low density housing for skilled working class households.

ABOVE: Raymond Unwin, champion of well-designed cottage housing for working class families.

The reputation of Parker and Unwin in garden city circles was established in connection with 3 major projects at New Earswick (from 1902), Letchworth (from 1903), and Hampstead Garden Suburb (from 1905). New Earswick was a model industrial village on the outskirts of York, sponsored by Joseph Rowntree. This development was essentially a test-bed for the development of new approaches to the design and layout of working class housing and supporting community facilities.[16] In addition to innovative forms of low density housing, the general plan for New Earswick provided for churches, shops, a library, a venue for social activities known as the 'folk hall' and a temperance inn.[17]

Letchworth presented a more complex set of challenges involving

ABOVE: Barry and Mabel Parker. (Garden City Collection, Letchworth Garden City Heritage Foundation)

RIGHT: Aerial view of Rowntree's model village at New Earswick.

BELOW RIGHT: New Earswick street scene.

NEW EARSWICK MODEL VILLAGE

THE MODEL VILLAGE NEW EARSWICK YORK

the application of Howard's concepts to create a functioning garden city. This project also allowed for the refinement of ideas about the design and layout of artisan housing. In the process a distinctive range of working class neighbourhoods was built on a co-partnership basis at Letchworth, known as Westholm Green, Eastholm Green, Bird's Hill and Pixmore.[18]

Hampstead Garden Suburb was conceived by Henrietta Barnett (1851–1936) as a model suburb for London. It was built in conjunction

VISIT OF HER MAJESTY THE QUEEN, THE PRINCE OF WALES, AND PRINCESS MARY
TO THE HAMPSTEAD GARDEN SUBURB ON FEBRUARY 26TH 1918.
FLATS IN ADDISON WAY, PROPERTY OF SECOND HAMPSTEAD TENANTS, LTD.

with the northern extension of Hampstead Heath. The project was intended to demonstrate how an enlightened suburban development could be achieved in a manner that respected the natural environment and provided healthful and attractive accommodation for people from all walks of life. At the proposal stage, many supporters of the garden city movement were reluctant to support any form of suburban development. In the event, Unwin decided to become involved in the project because he recognised that it was going to be extremely difficult

18. Ibid., pp. 82-3.

to make rapid progress in expanding the number of full-scale garden cities without strong backing from central government. Although the results at Hampstead Garden Suburb have often been criticised for the failure to provide accommodation for those on very low incomes, the artisan quarters designed by Parker and Unwin were a noteworthy achievement in the development of desirable housing for better-off working class households.

Raymond Unwin's ideas about housing design and layout were discussed in two major books published before WW1. The first, *The Art of Building a Home*, was a collection of essays jointly authored with Barry Parker which appeared in 1901. The second, *Town Planning in Practice*, was more wide-ranging in scope. It was written independently by Unwin and first appeared in 1909. In both cases, there was a clear underlying message that well-planned and well-constructed cottage accommodation should be available for all sections of society in urban and rural areas.[19]

Unwin strongly advocated the provision of single-family cottages with sizeable gardens, and was firmly convinced that flatted forms of accommodation were not an appropriate solution to the housing needs of families with children. In designing the recommended type of low density residential environments, it was particularly important to respect and take advantage of the natural conditions of the site.[20] This meant giving detailed attention to aspect (orientation to the sun), prospect (securing the best possible views for the main rooms), and landscape (positioning the house to adorn its immediate setting).[21] These principles were emphasised at a time when housing developers conventionally assumed that each new unit should face directly on to the street.[22]

With respect to site layout, Unwin argued for a flexible, cost-effective approach in designing local road networks, which provided opportunities for the creation of picturesque curving streetscapes.[23] He favoured imaginatively designed groups of cottages that promoted a sense of place and community, and took inspiration from both the Oxford quadrangles he had experienced as a youth and the rustic character of pre-industrial English villages. The desired types of working class cottages would ideally be arranged in short terraces within a cul-de-sac, or around a village green open on one side. Mindful of the need for economy, Unwin was also an early advocate of simplification and standardisation in the design and construction of working class housing.[24]

19. Aileen Reid, *Brentham – A History of the Pioneer Garden Suburb 1901–2001* (London, 2000), p. 42.

20. Swenarton, *Artisans and Architects*, p. 147.

21. Ibid.

22. Ibid.

23. Reid, *Brentham – A History of the Pioneer Garden Suburb 1901–2001*, pp. 45-6.

24. Swenarton, *Homes Fit for Heroes* (London, 1981), pp. 24-5.

With respect to residential density, Unwin went on record in 1907 as favouring an upper limit of 20 houses to the acre, net of roads and larger open spaces.[25] Wherever possible, however, the density of development should be reduced to a maximum of 12 houses to the acre in suburban areas and new garden cities and 8 houses to the acre in rural areas.[26] The recommended upper limit of 12 houses to the acre was necessary to ensure that the individual gardens would be large enough for the residents to grow food, either for their own consumption or for market gardening purposes to supplement the family income.

Regarding the internal planning of working class cottages, Unwin urged architects and developers to produce arrangements that were well thought out, with rooms of suitable size and shape for their intended functions.[27] In promoting imaginative layouts for short terraces, he favoured houses with relatively wide frontages of 20 feet or more and relatively shallow depths which still avoided the need for any rear projections. This basic form allowed for provision of a single spacious living room running the full depth of the house, with opportunities for windows at both front and back. Unwin felt that this arrangement had many advantages as a physical focus for family life, and clearly preferred it to the more traditional pattern of a less spacious living room with a separate parlour for special occasions.[28] In practice, however, these 'through and through' living rooms often did not prove to be highly popular when they were provided in future developments, since many of the residents apparently preferred a parlour. On the issue of internal space standards, Unwin contended that working class cottages should contain a minimum of 3 bedrooms, in order to allow for the growth of young families and to give mature households the option of a spare room for visitors.[29]

Towards the end of 1914, Raymond Unwin left private practice and accepted an appointment as Chief Town Planning Inspector for the Local Government Board.[30] His experience in designing new working class housing was to prove highly influential in shaping the future direction of national housing policy. Initially, he played a key role in expanding the supply of accommodation for civilian defence workers during WW1. During the closing stages of the war, through his participation in the work of the Tudor Walters Committee, he managed to place his personal imprint on the design guidance for local authority housing that was eventually to be built under the Housing and Town

25. Raymond Unwin, 'Cottage planning' in *First Garden City Limited, Where Shall I Live?* (London, 1907), p. 103.

26. Ibid.

27. Ibid., p. 104.

28. Reid, *Brentham – A History of the Pioneer Garden Suburb 1901–2001*, p. 44.

29. Unwin, 'Cottage planning', p. 107.

30. Miller, 'Raymond Unwin 1863–1940', p. 88.

ABOVE: Henry Vivian, driving force behind the development of tenant co-partnership schemes.

31. Ibid., p. 93.
32. Keith J. Skilleter, 'The role of public utility societies in early British town planning and housing reform', *Planning Perspectives*, 8, 1993, p. 132.

Planning Act of 1919. After leaving the civil service in 1928, he turned his attention to regional planning in his role as Technical Advisor to the Greater London Regional Planning Committee.[31]

HENRY VIVIAN AND CO-PARTNERSHIP HOUSING

The earliest developments of artisan housing at Letchworth and Hampstead Garden Suburb were sponsored by newly formed tenant co-partnership societies. These bodies were established to provide a hybrid form of tenure that attempted to combine various advantageous features of renting and owner-occupation. In practice, the operating principles of co-partnership societies were similar to those later adopted by equity-sharing co-operatives.

Tenant co-partnership societies provided a framework for resident participation and community identity. Within a given development, the occupants of the houses were regarded as tenants, although they were normally expected to help in meeting the overall capital requirements for the project. Each of the tenants made a rental payment for their home based on the particular characteristics of the property. In return for their additional capital contributions, they were entitled to share in any future increases in the financial value of the entire development. The ownership interests of the local residents were directly linked to the overall success of the development rather than to the price that could be obtained for a given individual property. Relative to conventional methods of speculative development, the application of co-partnership principles focused greater attention on the collective needs of residents and the provision of community facilities. In legal terms, tenant co-partnership organisations were eligible to register as public utility societies, which then placed them in a position to apply for loan finance from the Public Works Loan Board.

The earliest examples of co-partnership housing, dating from the mid-1880s, were implemented in the London area. Between 1900 and 1914 the tenant co-partnership movement expanded to other parts of Britain and the physical results were generally seen to be impressive. By 1914 around 30 co-partnership societies were actively providing housing in a variety of locations.[32] Many of these organisations had links with the garden city movement and were consciously attempting to set new standards for artisan housing.[33] Unfortunately the growth of tenant co-partnership societies was interrupted by the war and the pre-1914 momentum was not sustained. The more experienced tenant co-partnership societies found it difficult to complete their intended developments in the economic conditions of the early 1920s. Although various attempts were made after WW1 to stimulate new housing developments by public utility societies and other voluntary organisations, the available financial assistance from central government was not seen to be sufficiently generous to compensate for the unusually high level of construction costs.

Henry Vivian (1868–1930) was the leading proponent of co-partnership housing. A native of Devon, Vivian was initially trained by his father as a carpenter and took up a formal apprenticeship in Plymouth at the age of 16.[34] Two years later he moved to London, where he became involved in trade union activities and the wider co-operative movement. In 1890, he was appointed as secretary of the Labour Association for Promoting Co-operative Production Amongst the Workforce. This splinter group within the co-operative movement was committed to principles of profit-sharing.[35] Subsequently, in 1906, he was elected to Parliament as a Lib-Lab candidate for Birkenhead and managed to retain this seat until the general election of December 1910.

In his efforts to promote co-partnership principles in housing, Henry Vivian was extending the pioneering work of E. O. Greening and Benjamin Jones and the examples that had been set by Tenant Co-operators Ltd in South London, East London and Surrey during the mid-1880s.[36] Vivian managed to make significant progress in 1901, when he played a leading role in establishing Ealing Tenants Ltd which went on to develop Brentham Garden Suburb. Apparently, at the outset, there was no formal link with the garden city movement. As noted by Aileen Reid,

33. S. Martin Gaskell, 'The suburb salubrious: town planning in practice' in Anthony Sutcliffe (ed.), *British Town Planning: the formative years* (Leicester, 1981), pp. 29-30.

34. Reid, *Brentham – A History of the Pioneer Garden Suburb 1901–2001*, p. 21.

35. Ibid., p. 17.

36. Ibid., pp. 23-4.

BELOW: Listing of office bearers and executive committee of Co-partnership Tenants' Housing Council.

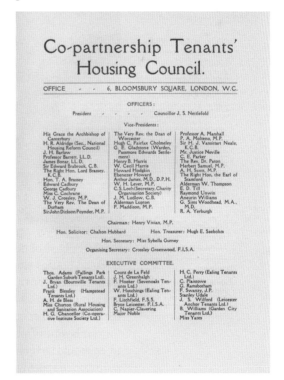

RIGHT: The Institute, a major community facility provided at Brentham Garden Suburb by Ealing Tenants Ltd.

BELOW: Interesting corner development in Fowlers Walk, Brentham Garden Suburb.

37. Ibid, p. 65.
38. Ibid., p. 138.
39. Ibid., pp. 141-2.

EALING GARDEN SUBURB, THE INSTITUTE.

the first phase of development involved fairly long rows of well-built terraced houses sited along straight roads.[37] By 1906, additional land was required for the next phase of development and Ealing Tenants Ltd acquired a sizable parcel adjacent to the current site.[38] At this stage, the firm of Parker and Unwin was appointed to prepare an overall plan for the layout of new streets, which also designated where existing trees should be retained and new provisions made for public buildings, shops, open space and other recreational facilities.[39] A number of other

ABOVE: Artistic impression of Letchworth co-partnership housing by Frank Dean.

architects were involved in designing the additional housing, including F. Cavendish Pearson and G. Lister Sutcliffe. By 1913, a total 510 houses had been built at Brentham Garden Suburb and the area had taken on a decidedly garden city character.

In order to encourage the growth of tenant co-partnership societies, Henry Vivian established two types of supporting organisations. A body called the Co-partnership Tenants Housing Council was formed in 1905, as a vehicle for the general promotion of co-partnership principles in housing.[40] Two years later, a second body called Co-partnership Tenants Ltd was created through a federation of individual societies, for the purpose of providing advice and back-up services to member organisations on important matters such as raising financial capital, procuring building materials, and recruiting skilled professionals.[41] Vivian served as chairman of Co-partnership Tenants Ltd and Raymond Unwin served as its consulting architect.

The extent to which tenant co-partnership societies had spread to various parts of England by 1913 is apparent from the following list of member organisations involved in the work of the Co-partnership Tenants Ltd at that date:[42]

40. Co-partnership Tenants Housing Council, Garden Suburbs, Villages & Homes, (London, 1906).

41. Reid, *Brentham – A History of the Pioneer Garden Suburb 1901–2001*, p. 77.

42. Skilleter, 'The role of public utility societies in early British town planning and housing reform', p. 136.

RIGHT: Co-partnership housing at Burnage Garden Village, Manchester.

BELOW: Co-partnership housing at Penkhull Garden Village, Stoke-on-Trent.

Anchor Tenants Ltd (Humberstone, Leicester; formed in 1902)
Sevenoaks Tenants Ltd (Sevenoaks, Kent; 1903)
Garden City Tenants Ltd (Letchworth, Hertfordshire; 1904)
Manchester Tenants Ltd (Burnage; 1906)
Oldham Garden Suburb Tenants Ltd (Hollis Green; 1906)
Warrington Tenants Ltd (Great Sankey and Grappenhall; 1906)
Fallings Park Garden Suburb Tenants Ltd (Wolverhampton; 1907)
Hampstead Tenants Ltd (Hampstead Garden Suburb; 1907)
Harborne Tenants Ltd (Moor Pool, Birmingham; 1907)

LIVERPOOL GARDEN SUBURB SUMMER FESTIVAL. 1913.   Photo. W. Pighling

Stoke-on-Trent Tenants Ltd (Penkhull; 1908)

Derwentwater Tenants Ltd (Greta Hamlet, Keswick; 1909)

Second Hampstead Tenants Ltd (Hampstead Garden Suburb; 1909)

Liverpool Tenants Ltd (Wavertree; 1910)

Sealand Tenants Ltd (Queensferry, Cheshire; 1910)

Hampstead Heath Extension Tenants Ltd
        (Hampstead Garden Suburb; 1912)

Oakwood Tenants Ltd (Hampstead Garden Suburb; 1913)

A number of other co-partnership societies were associated with the garden city movement, but had chosen not to become formal members of Co-partnership Tenants Ltd.[43] From the information provided in publications of the Garden City Association, there were additional co-partnership developments within England at Bournville, Coventry, Didsbury (Manchester), Fairfield (Manchester), Haslemere (Surrey), Knebworth (Hertfordshire), New Eltham (London Borough of Greenwich), Newby West (Carlisle), Sutton (Surrey), and Worcester. Additional developments of this type were noted in Wales at Caerphilly, Fforestfach, Llanidloes, Machynlleth, Merthyr Tydfil, Rhiwbina (Cardiff), Wrexham and Ynysybwl. A number of similar initiatives were also under way in Scotland before the outbreak of WW1 which are discussed in Chapter 4.

43. These additional co-partnership developments have been identified from two sources: Ewart G. Culpin, *The Garden City Movement Up-To-Date* (London, 1914) and Margaret Tims, Ealing Tenants Ltd, Ealing Local History Society, Members' Papers, No. 8, 1966.
44. Hardy, *From Garden Cities to New Towns*, p. 95.
45. Ibid., p. 100.
46. Ibid., p. 101.
47. Ewart G. Culpin, *The Garden City Movement Up-To-Date*, p. 2.

EVOLVING AIMS OF THE GARDEN CITY ASSOCIATION

As First Garden City Ltd proceeded with the development of Letchworth, the Garden City Association carried on with its campaigning activities. During the remaining years before the outbreak of WW1, the reform agenda of the Garden City Association was adapted and broadened to promote the case for regional planning, proper control over town extension, better design of suburban housing, decentralisation of industry, regeneration of rural areas, and preservation of the countryside.

In pursuing this set of policy objectives, working relationships and alliances were built with organisations that shared these concerns, such as the National Housing Reform Council, the Royal Institute of British Architects, the Cities Committee of the Sociological Society and the newly formed Town Planning Institute. As discussed more fully in Chapter 3, the relationship with the National Housing Reform Council proved to be particularly important in Scotland, both in promoting garden city housing and in stimulating debate about the relative advantages of providing tenements or cottages for working class families. The National Housing Reform Council was founded in 1900, and renamed the National Housing and Town Planning Council in 1909. Two figures were largely responsible for the development of this body – Alderman

William Thompson of Richmond Borough Town Council and Henry R. Aldridge who served as Secretary from his home base in Leicester.

During this formative period, the Garden City Association also managed to build an international network of people and organisations interested in Howard's ideas. This network was promoted through various types of activity at home and abroad. The first gathering of the International Garden City Congress was held in London during the summer of 1904.[44] This event attracted delegates from Germany, France and the United States. Thereafter, a series of study visits was organised to provide opportunities for garden city enthusiasts to observe various developments that were of mutual interest. Visits were organised to Continental locations for the benefit of British delegates and tours to British locations for the benefit of Continental delegates. In 1913, the International Garden Cities and Town Planning Association was launched to support the growth of new initiatives in other countries.[45] Whilst this work was interrupted by the outbreak of the war, an initial congress did take place in London with accompanying site visits to other parts of England.[46]

Once the garden city style of housing at Letchworth and Hampstead Garden Suburb had gained national acclaim, many commercial housebuilders began to describe their more conventional suburban developments as 'garden cities'. Since the Garden City Association regarded the general standard of suburban development to be highly unsatisfactory, an attempt was made to clarify what the organisation considered to be proper definitions of the terms 'garden city', 'garden suburb' and 'garden village'. In a 1914 publication, the organisation defined these terms for the benefit of the wider public as follows:[47]

> A 'Garden City' is a self-contained town, industrial, agricultural, residential – planned as a whole – and occupying land to provide garden-surrounded homes for at least 30,000 persons, as well as a wide belt of open fields. It combines the advantages of town and country, and prepares the way for a national movement, stemming the tide of the population now leaving the countryside and sweeping into our overcrowded cities.
>
> A 'Garden Suburb' provides that the normal growth of existing

ABOVE: Alderman William Thompson of Richmond Borough Town Council, leading figure in the work of the National Housing and Town Planning Council.

ABOVE: Henry R. Aldridge, Secretary, National Housing and Town Planning Council.

cities shall be along healthy lines; and when such cities are not already too large, such suburbs are most useful, and even in the case of overgrown London they may be, though on the other hand they tend to drive the country yet further afield, and do not deal with the root evil – rural depopulation.

'Garden Villages', such as Bournville and Port Sunlight, are Garden Cities in miniature, but depend upon some neighbouring city for water, light and drainage; they have not the valuable provision of a protective belt, and are usually the centre of one great industry only.

GROWTH IN LOCAL AUTHORITY COTTAGE PROVISION

In Great Britain and Ireland between 1880 and 1914 some important precedents in cottage building accommodation were set by local authorities. The most interesting examples in Britain were located in what are now regarded as inner-suburban neighbourhoods of larger cities and towns. The most important precedents in Ireland were in rural areas. A number of significant examples also appeared in Scotland, particularly in Lanarkshire, which are discussed in Chapter 4.

The suburban examples were mainly undertaken by a small number of progressive local authorities in England. These initiatives were generally intended to demonstrate how the design deficiencies of late-Victorian 'bye-law' terraced housing could be overcome. In various respects the results were influenced by the earlier experience of non-profit housing trusts dating from the mid-1870s. The most impressive examples of pre-1914 local authority cottage provision, such as the outstanding work carried out by London County Council (LCC), can be seen as a transition towards the wider application of garden city principles. At this stage, there were limits to what progressive local authorities could achieve through direct provision, given the continuing absence of any form of central government subsidisation under the Housing Acts. In general, the initial local authority cottage developments were built at densities of 25 to 30 units per acre, still double the upper limit recommended by Raymond Unwin for garden city housing in suburban locations.

Alderman William Thompson of Richmond Borough Town Council was a staunch advocate of local authority cottage provision as well as a leading figure in the National Housing Reform Council. Under his stewardship, the Borough of Richmond was among the first group of authorities (along with Birmingham, Huddersfield and Llandudno) to promote cottage building for general needs under Part 3 of the 1890 Housing of the Working Classes Act.[48] Alderman Thompson was personally associated with the development known as Richmond Cottages, which was formally approved in 1893 by the Local Government Board.[49]

This development was situated within easy walking distance of 3 suburban rail stations, in a popular working class neighbourhood south of the River Thames. The first phase of construction involved a mix of 62 terraced houses and 2-storey cottage flats on 2.5 acres of land. Most of the properties were located along a newly-built straight road leading off a busy main thoroughfare. Although the housing tended to be grouped in short terraces, little attention was given to either picturesque details or innovations in site layout.

In architectural and site planning terms, the most creative early examples of suburban local authority estates were built by the LCC from 1903 to 1915. These developments were designed by a talented team of young professionals in the Housing Branch of the LCC Architects' Department, who were strongly influenced by ideas associated with the arts and crafts and garden city movements. Key examples of their work included the Totterdown Fields estate at Tooting, the White Hart Lane estate at Tottenham, the Norbury estate at Croydon, and the Old Oak estate at Hammersmith.[50] These relatively large projects ranged in size from 330 units, in the case of Old Oak, to 1,260 units, in the case of Totterdown Fields. Faced with stringent budget constraints, the team made a genuine attempt to design attractive residential environments with interesting variations in house size and physical details. Although financial limitations would not allow for the wide-fronted terraced houses favoured by Raymond Unwin, the youthful architects of the Housing Branch did manage to avoid extensive rear projections.[51] Garden city design principles were most evident in the Old Oak estate, where the site layout provided for a number of curving streets and deep quadrangles.

48. Alderman W. Thompson, *Housing of the Working Classes* (Richmond, Surrey, 1899), pp. 43-5.
49. Ibid., p. 23.
50. See Susan Beattie, *A Revolution in London Housing* (London, 1980).
51. London County Council, *Housing of the Working Classes in London* (London, 1913), p. 72.

The Irish experience, largely in rural areas, is important to mention for reasons relating to the number of cottages built and the innovative arrangements for central government subsidisation. Between 1880 and 1914, nearly 50,000 cottages were built by rural authorities under statutory provisions of the Irish Labourers Acts.[52] During the initial phase of cottage building to 1906, central government was only prepared to help with the provision of loan finance. Over this 25-year period, 20,000 cottages were constructed mainly along roadsides in close proximity to places of work. In the 8 years that followed to 1914, as many as 30,000 cottages were built for agricultural labourers, in somewhat larger concentrations on the fringe of urban settlements. This significant increase in the volume of construction was directly linked to the availability of a central government subsidy covering one-third of approved development costs. Although these modest cottages were usually designed in a utilitarian manner, the sheer numbers produced in response to the availability of central government financial assistance was duly noted by housing reformers who looked to the state to expand its role in the provision of working class accommodation.

52. Murray Fraser, *John Bull's Other Houses* (Liverpool, 1996), p. 28.
53. Charles E. Allan and Francis J. Allan, *The Housing of the Working Classes Acts, 1890–1909 and the Housing Acts, 1914* (London, 1916), 4th Edition, pp. 287-90.
54. Ibid.

HOUSING AND THE WAR EFFORT

Once Britain had declared war with Germany on 4th August 1914, various measures were taken at central government level to increase the supply of available housing for civilian defence workers. Initially, Parliament approved the Housing Act of 1914, which was specifically aimed at providing additional accommodation for civilian defence workers that were either employed directly, or on behalf of, a central government department.[53] As originally passed, this legislation enabled the necessary housing to be developed through two alternative approaches. One option was for the Local Government Board to commission a registered public utility society to build a given number of houses in a specified location, with any permanent accommodation ideally provided on a tenant co-partnership basis.[54] The other alternative was for the Commissioner of Works, after due consultation with the Local Government Board, to acquire a site directly and organise the construction process on behalf of a particular central government department.[55] Whichever of these methods was used, it was necessary to obtain Treasury consent for each new development built for this purpose.

At the outset, it was recognised that a flexible funding framework would be needed to minimise delays and avoid financial haggling. Despite the urgency of the situation, the new legislation failed to provide an improved funding regime for public utility societies, although local authorities were encouraged to help in bringing any authorised developments to fruition. Where the anticipated rental charges for a given project could not reasonably be expected to cover the full range of development costs, the Treasury was empowered to provide a capital grant on a discretionary basis.[56] In the event, this funding mechanism failed to generate an adequate level of response. On the home front, conditions within the building industry soon became problematic. Faced with rising costs and shortages of labour and materials, potential sponsors of co-partnership developments found it difficult to rise to the challenge. In a matter of months it was obvious that other approaches would be essential to meet central government targets in different parts of Britain.

Within government circles, opinions varied as to whether the housing constructed for civilian defence workers should be temporary or permanent. Initially, temporary forms of construction were considered to be advantageous on cost grounds. Before long, however, it was recognised that there was little difference in the costs of land and infrastructure for temporary or permanent types of construction, and that availability of building materials was the key issue in producing the necessary accommodation. Under wartime conditions, it became impossible to replenish stocks of imported timber which was often an essential component of temporary housing. This situation produced a shift toward permanent forms of construction, which in turn encouraged the application of garden city ideas in meeting these needs. Campaigning bodies with an interest in housing and town planning reform urged the government to address this problem by consciously setting new standards for working class provision based on garden city principles.

By the end of 1914, Raymond Unwin had accepted an appointment as Chief Town Planning Inspector at the Local Government Board.[57] During the course of the war, he managed to serve in various capacities that allowed him to promote low density housing in the garden city style

55. Ibid.
56. Swenarton, *Homes Fit for Heroes*, p. 52.
57. Miller, 'Raymond Unwin 1863–1940', p. 88.

for civilian defence workers in numerous locations throughout Great Britain. In many cases, these new developments were built directly by a central government agency, such as the Ministry of Munitions or the Local Government Board. However, additional developments were often constructed through a partnership approach based on collaboration between the Local Government Board and various private employers in key defence industries.

In July 1915, Unwin was seconded to the explosives division of the Ministry of Munitions where he was placed in charge of an ambitious programme of factory construction and housebuilding.[58] The housing elements of this work involved a range of accommodation including temporary hostels for 20,000 single workers (mainly women), temporary cottages for 2800 families, and 10,000 permanent houses on 38 different sites in various parts of the country.[59] In a number of instances, the developments of permanent housing were intended as benchmarks for the improvement of living conditions after the war.

The first development of permanent housing within the Ministry of Munitions programme was begun in early 1915, about 6 months before Unwin's secondment. Known as the Well Hall estate, it was a major development located at Eltham in Kent to ease the pressures on the local supply of housing that were generated by the rapid expansion of the Woolwich Arsenal workforce. At the outset, the general aim was to provide a minimum of 1000 houses, using the architectural services of the Office of Works.[60] One of the Principal Architects at the Office of Works, Frank Baines, was placed in charge of the design and layout of the Well Hall estate to be built on a 96-acre site. During the 1890s, Baines had served an apprenticeship with C. R. Ashbee, a leading figure in the English arts and crafts movement.[61] He was determined to create a desirable picturesque living environment in the face of urgent directives for a speedy response.[62] In the event, nearly 1,300 dwellings were constructed in less than a full year, but a high price was paid for this accommodation in economic terms. The outturn costs for the Well Hall estate were more than double the original estimate.[63]

The housing stock at Well Hall consisted mainly of cottages with 3 or 4 bedrooms, designed as either semi-detached properties or relatively short terraces of 3 to 15 units.[64] About 15 per cent were built in the form of 2-storey cottage flats, with each flat containing 2 bedrooms.[65] These cottage flats were introduced at a late stage in the construction

58. Ibid., p. 88.
59. Swenarton, *Homes Fit for Heroes*, p. 51.
60. Ibid., p. 53.
61. Ibid., p. 56.
62. Ibid., p. 55.
63. Swenarton, *Homes Fit for Heroes*, p. 55.
64. Ibid., p. 55.
65. Ibid.

LEFT: Ministry of Munitions Well Hall Estate at Eltham, Royal Borough of Greenwich.

66. Ibid.
67. Ibid.

process, largely as an economy measure to help in restraining the cost overrun.[66] This decision proved to be a source of tension between Unwin and Baines, with Unwin expressing his long-held view that flats of any description were not really suitable for family living. Baines, in response, contended that the cottage flats at Well Hall had proved popular, and in his next project for aircraft workers at Roe Green Garden Village in the London Borough of Brent he decided to raise the share of cottage flats to 40 per cent.[67]

When the Well Hall estate was first completed, it received a good deal of comment in the press – both favourable and unfavourable. The high standard of accommodation was generally praised, but the excessive costs of construction were regarded as unacceptable. In architectural and town planning circles, the Well Hall experience was seen to highlight the need for simplification of design and standardisation of construction and to raise questions about the complete lack of attention given to the provision of schools, churches, shops and other community facilities for a community of 1,300 households.

During the war years a group of architects and town planners based at the University of Liverpool were leading proponents of simplification and standardisation in Britain. This group, which included key figures such as Charles Reilly, Stanley Adshead and Patrick Abercrombie, generally favoured a 'neo-Georgian' approach to design and strongly opposed the garden city

RIGHT: Aerial view of Roe Green Garden Village.

BELOW: Cottage flats at Roe Green Garden Village, in Goldsmith Lane.

ROE GREEN *from the Air.*

68. Simon Pepper and Mark Swenarton, 'Home fronts' in Mark Swenarton, *Building the New Jerusalem* (Bracknell, 2008), p. 28.
69. Ibid.

movement's efforts to recapture the traditional character of pre-industrial English villages.[68] What was needed, from the standpoint of the Liverpool group, was a more disciplined urban aesthetic based on the 'lesser domestic architecture of the 18th century'.[69] As Mark Swenarton has observed:

> . . . the Liverpool group called for a sober style of design which relied for its effect, not on picturesque detail and idiosyncratic individuality, but on proportion, repetition and similarity. In-

spiration, they said, should be sought from the Georgian period, when a restful and satisfying overall effect had been obtained by the repetition of simple blocks with carefully placed and proportioned doors and windows.[70]

Towards the end of WW1, the Liverpool group had an opportunity to design Dormanstown Village, near Redcar on the Yorkshire coast, as a demonstration of the superiority of the neo-Georgian approach. This development, designed by the firm of Adshead, Ramsay and Abercrombie, was intended for employees based at the local Dormans Long steelworks. In many respects, the basic layout for the new village of Dormanstown was inspired by the formal geometry of late 18th and early 19th century town extension schemes.[71] The various buildings, which had little in the way of decorative features, were placed on the site within an axial pattern of main roads.[72] Between 1917 and 1920, 340 single-family cottages were provided along with schools, churches, a market square and other community facilities. A patented method known as The 'Dorlonco' system, involving the bolting of concrete slabs on to steel frames, was used to build a portion of the housing stock.[73] After the war, a number of local authorities opted to use this non-traditional method of construction, but the results proved to be generally unpopular with tenants due to problems of condensation, dampness and poor sound insulation.[74]

BELOW: Axial planning at Dormanstown, Redcar, Yorkshire.

70. Swenarton, *Homes Fit for Heroes*, p. 63.
71. Simon Pepper and Mark Swenarton, 'Neo-Georgian maison-type' in Mark Swenarton, *Building the New Jerusalem*, pp. 31-2.
72. Ibid.
73. Nigel Alan Robins, *Homes for Heroes* (Swansea, 1992), p. 56.
74. Ibid.

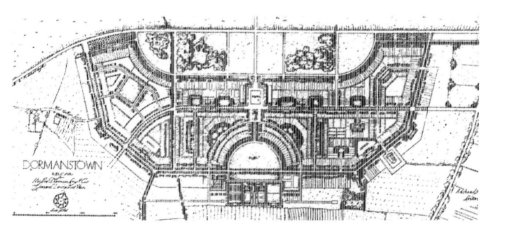

RIGHT: 'Neo-Georgian' houses built on the 'Dorlonco' steel frame system at Dormanstown.

ELECTORAL PLEDGES TO BUILD HOMES FIT FOR HEROES

During the course of WW1 social unrest was evident in many places of work throughout Britain. There were also numerous conflicts on the home front related to housing conditions. Apart from the new developments for civilian defence workers, housing construction was virtually suspended for the duration of the war. Shortages of accommodation appeared in many communities, along with problems of lack of maintenance, rising rents and illegal evictions. In Glasgow and a number of other cities, the militant responses of local tenants were instrumental in pressuring for the introduction of a national system of rent control in 1915.

As the war appeared to be drawing to a close and victory seemed assured, the political outlook in Britain was extremely uncertain with an early general election anticipated. Much of the uncertainty about the outcome of the general election was linked to the impact of electoral reform. With the passage of the Representation of the People Act of 1918, a total of 8 million new voters (including 6 million women and 2 million men) were eligible to cast their ballots for the first time. Social unrest on the Continent, especially the threat of revolution in Russia and Germany, also contributed to the widely held feelings of uncertainty and insecurity. As previously noted, once the electoral campaign was under way, David Lloyd George struck a chord with audiences by recognising an urgent need for national policies to improve the living conditions of ordinary citizens. In this context, the catchphrases 'A Land Fit for

Heroes to Live In' and 'Homes Fit for Heroes' became rallying cries for a peaceful path to British social reconstruction.

With the return of military personnel to civilian life, the housing shortages in many parts of the country became more acute. Although an increase in housebuilding, especially for working class households, was clearly needed, significant difficulties were emerging in the construction industry. Labour and materials were both in short supply, and the average construction costs for a 3-bedroom house had tripled since 1914. Until such time as 'normal' peacetime conditions were restored to the construction sector of the economy, there seemed to be little prospect of major investment in housing by private developers, particularly for the benefit of working class families. Although the current predicament was expected to be temporary, the key to the return of commercial incentives for new housebuilding was a substantial decrease in the level of construction costs. How quickly this might happen was both difficult to predict and heavily dependent upon whether any effective policies to regulate conditions in the construction sector might materialise.

In July 1918, a Committee was appointed by the President of the Local Government Board to consider appropriate standards for the construction of new working class housing. Sir John Tudor Walters (1868–1933), the Liberal Member of Parliament for Sheffield Brightside, chaired this Committee which was initially given a remit to examine 'questions of building construction in connection with the provision of dwellings for the working classes in England and Wales, and report upon methods of securing economy and despatch in the provision of such dwellings'.[75] Tudor Walters was trained as an architect and 3 other architects were appointed as members of the Committee – Frank Baines, Raymond Unwin and Sir Aston Webb. Nine months after the formation of the Committee the official remit was amended to include Scotland and J. Walker Smith, the Chief Engineer and Controller of Housing and Town Planning at the Local Government Board for Scotland, was added to the panel.[76]

The final report of the Tudor Walters Committee was published in November 1918. The Committee chose to interpret its remit widely and the end product is generally regarded as the first comprehensive treatise on the political, technical and practical issues involved in the design of the small house.[77] According to Mark Swenarton, Raymond Unwin was the principal author of the report and the driving force in defining the key policy recommendations.[78] In performing this role,

75. Cd. 9191, Report of the Committee to Consider Questions of Building Construction in Connection with the Provision of Dwellings of the Working Classes in England and Wales, and Scotland (Tudor Walters Report), 1918, p. 3.

76. Swenarton, *Homes Fit for Heroes*, p. 93.

77. Swenarton, *Homes Fit for Heroes*, pp. 93-4.

78. Ibid., p. 96.

ABOVE: Sir John Tudor Walters
MP.

79. Cd. 9191, pp. 4-8.

he was able to draw on his extensive experience in both the garden city movement and the wartime efforts to provide housing for civilian defence workers.

Two of the key elements within the report were concerned with the desired standards for a national programme of housebuilding to increase the supply of working class accommodation and the type of administrative arrangements that were seen to be needed to ensure that these standards would be met. The report opened with a statement about the nature of the housing problem and its potential solution.[79] The existing shortages of living accommodation were thought to be a by-product of both the long-term decline of working class housing construction before the war and the virtual cessation of speculative housebuilding during the war. On the basis of estimates prepared by local authorities, at least 500,000 new dwellings were seen to be needed to ease the shortages in England, Wales and Scotland. However, there were likely to be problems in meeting even this minimum figure unless effective action was taken at central government level to regulate the transition from wartime to peacetime conditions within the economy and to ensure that a sufficient supply of labour and materials would be available to facilitate a national housing drive.

During the course of the Committee's investigations, many local authorities had indicated a willingness to develop working class housing if an adequate level of financial assistance was made available by central government. Given the substantial amount of new building that was seen to be urgently required, it was felt that any contributions by local authorities would need to be supplemented by the efforts of public utility societies and private developers.

If local authorities were to be expected to play a major part in removing the prevailing shortages, significant changes in the traditional pattern of relations between central and local government agencies would be required. In the view of the Committee, the role of the Local Government Boards needed to be strengthened in order to co-ordinate and supervise the responses of local authorities. Although the final report did not contain any explicit references to garden city design principles, there was a clear statement to the effect that any new housing developments in urban locations should be built on outlying sites covered by approved town planning schemes. The sites in question would require to be well served by tramways and other means of transport, and the desired forms of low density housing would need to be designed by competent architects and supported by a range of local services and amenities that were essential for the development of healthy communities.

The more technical sections of the report were concerned with the principles of site layout, the internal planning of working class dwellings, and the case for achieving economies through standardisation and non-traditional methods of construction. Many of these findings were later incorporated within the official guidance issued by central government for the development of new working class housing under the provisions of the Housing and Town Planning Act of 1919.

HOUSING AND TOWN PLANNING ACT OF 1919

The general election held in December 1918 resulted in a Coalition government headed up by David Lloyd George. Seven months later, Parliament passed new legislation in the fields of housing and town planning that was intended to provide a framework for an effective response to the national housing shortage. In a number of respects, the Housing and Town Planning Act of 1919 (which applied to England and Wales) and its Scottish counterpart (known as the Housing and Town Planning (Scotland) Act of 1919) represented a significant departure from the earlier framework of Victorian housing legislation which generally empowered local authorities to take certain types of action if they were so inclined but did not offer any form of subsidisation from central government.

Under the amended statutory framework local authorities were expected to assume a more pro-active role in meeting the various housing needs within their areas. Whereas previously local authorities were *permitted* to respond to the problems at hand, they were now *required* to ensure that effective measures were being taken to address the situation, either by the local authority itself or by other competent parties. This new obligation for local authorities in the housing field was to be carried out under the general supervision of central government. Initially, the Local Government Boards were given the responsibility for administering the Housing and Town Planning Act of 1919 Act. Following a reorganisation of central government in 1920 this function was transferred to the Ministry of Health in England and Wales and the Scottish Board of Health in Scotland.

Given the high level of residential construction costs, financial assistance from central government was recognised as essential in achieving the desired volume of general needs housebuilding for working class households, at least until such time as 'normal' conditions returned to the building industry. The subsidy provisions adopted under the 1919 Act were contentious, since a maximum contribution was defined for local authorities but the potential contribution from central government was virtually open-ended. In England and Wales, local authorities were expected to help in covering any operating losses on their new housing developments by making a maximum payment equivalent to one-penny-in-the-pound on the rates. In Scotland, the maximum contribution by local authorities was limited to the equivalent of four-fifths-of-a-penny-in-the-pound on the rates.

Close central government supervision over the development process was deemed to be necessary for several reasons. Many local authorities had very limited experience in direct housing provision and a substantial level of financial support from the Treasury was anticipated. Moreover, central government was anxious to ensure that appropriate standards of design and construction were met. The approval process for any new 1919 Act developments was administered in 7 stages. Initially the local authority was required to assess the number of additional houses needed to remove any shortage of accommodation in the area.[80] Once this figure had been mutually agreed with central government, for each development, it was necessary to obtain approval for the site location, the acquisition price for the land, the general layout of the houses, the terms of borrowing for streets and sewers, and the range of internal plans for the houses to be provided.[81] Before proceeding to the construction stage, the winning tender and the proposed rental charges also needed to be sanctioned by central government.[82]

In the face of chaotic conditions within the building industry, local authorities generally found it difficult to meet their agreed housebuilding targets. Prior to the Armistice, the Ministry of Reconstruction had appointed a committee to consider the types of problems that might constrain the post-war housing drive. According to the findings of this committee, two things were essential to avoid any serious impediments to the rate of progress. It would be necessary to continue the wartime

80. Robins, *Homes for Heroes*, p. 27.
81. Ibid.
82. Ibid.

controls on construction activity and to give clear priority in the allocation of labour and materials to the elimination of housing shortages
across the country. However, this advice was subsequently ignored by
the more powerful Cabinet Demobilisation Committee and the wartime
controls on the building industry were eventually dismantled.[83]

Somewhat unexpectedly, the British economy remained fairly buoyant until the autumn of 1920, but the volume of housing construction
was well below the official target of 500,000 new dwellings over a 3-year
period. The economy took a turn for the worse during 1921, and the
generous subsidy regime for local authority housebuilding was withdrawn in mid-July as part of a wider package of public expenditure cuts.[84]

Under the provisions of the Housing and Town Planning Act of
1919, English and Welsh local authorities managed to build a total of
170,000 units and Scottish local authorities managed to complete an
additional 25,000 units. Although the number of completions was
clearly disappointing the physical character of the new local authority
developments was often impressive. The 1919 Act developments were
generally produced along garden city lines, in accordance with central
government design guidance, at density levels of around 12 units to the
acre in urban areas and 8 units to the acre in rural areas.

In England and Wales, priority was normally given to larger family
houses with 3 or more bedrooms.[85] Class 'A' houses containing 3 bedrooms but no parlour were expected to provide a living room with a
minimum floor space of 180 square feet, a scullery (minimum 80 ft²), a
larder (minimum 12 ft²), a coal store (minimum 15 ft²), a first bedroom
(minimum 150 ft²), a second bedroom (minimum 100 ft²), and a third
bedroom (minimum 65 ft²).[86] Class 'B' houses containing 3 bedrooms
with a parlour were designed to provide an additional room on the
ground floor of not less than 120 square feet.[87] Each of these house
types was required to have a fixed bath within a separate compartment,
a water closet positioned under suitable cover, and a hot water supply
to both bath and sink.[88]

Throughout Britain, during the relatively brief period when the
Housing and Town Planning Act of 1919 was in force, the main objective of national housing policy was to remove the existing shortages
of accommodation by expanding the supply of 'general needs' housing
that was available for working class households. The best of the 1919
Act developments succeeded in setting new standards for working class

83. Cd. 9197, Report of the
Committee Appointed by the
Minister of Reconstruction
to Consider the Position of
the Building Industry after
the War, 1918. This Committee was chaired by Sir James
Carmichael.
84. Swenarton, *Homes Fit for
Heroes*, pp. 112-5.
85. Local Government Board,
Manual on the Preparation
of State-Aided Housing
Schemes (London, 1919),
Appendix IV, p. 29.
86. Ibid.
87. Ibid.
88. Ibid., p. 9.

housing in many parts of the country. These low density houses in the garden city style have come to be seen as the physical embodiment of the 'Homes Fit for Heroes' idea. Although the official housebuilding targets were never realised in quantitative terms, and the rent levels were usually well beyond the reach of unskilled workers and poorer sections of the population, these areas built by local authorities have generally remained very popular places to live over the years and have been well cared for by generations of residents. Ironically, these properties are now overwhelmingly owner-occupied as a result of the Right-to-Buy legislation introduced in the 1980s.

A PLEA FOR MORE GARDEN CITIES

Amidst the calls for action to deal with the national housing shortage, there was a strong possibility that Howard's vision for full-scale garden cities would be ignored if not forgotten. Letchworth was still regarded by Howard's followers as the only genuine effort to create a proper garden city. In an attempt to keep Howard's ideas before the general public, a talented group of garden city supporters, including C. B. Purdom, Frederic Osborn, Patrick Abercrombie and G. D. H. Cole, decided to restate the case for developing additional self-contained settlements.[89] A short publication called *New Towns after the War* (and sub-titled '*an argument for Garden Cities*') was produced in 1918 with a view to influencing the general direction of national policy.[90] The text was known to have been drafted by Frederic Osborn, although he was not specifically identified as its author.[91]

New Towns after the War was an ambitious plea for as many as 100 self-contained settlements. The main departures from Howard's original vision were suggestions that central government should prepare a national strategy for the creation of garden cities and then take measures to create a suitable framework for implementation.[92] Although the publication of *New Towns after the War* made little immediate impact, Osborn continued to promote the basic set of ideas throughout the inter-war period and eventually came to play a major part in conceptualising the British New Towns programme during the late 1930s.

89. Hardy, *From Garden Cities to New Towns*, p. 127.
90. 'New Townsmen', *New Towns after the War* (London, 1918).
91. Hardy, *From Garden Cities to New Towns*, p. 127.
92. Hardy, *From Garden Cities to New Towns*, p. 128.

LAUNCH OF WELWYN GARDEN CITY

Despite the many problems encountered in the development of Letchworth, Ebenezer Howard remained convinced that voluntary initiative offered the best way forward for the garden city movement. After the war he began to look for a viable opportunity for the creation of a second garden city.[93] Largely through his personal effort, Welwyn Garden City was launched in 1920.[94] A temporary company, known as Second Garden City Ltd, was set up in October 1919 for the purpose of finding a suitable site, with Frederic Osborn serving as Secretary.[95] By the end of April 1920, a large swathe of agricultural land had been secured about 20 miles north of London, near Hatfield station, and Welwyn Garden City Ltd had been set up to take the project to the construction stage.[96] After an initial bout of optimism, it proved extremely difficult to make rapid progress in achieving the original vision for the second garden city.

Initially a target population of 40,000 to 50,000 was envisaged for Welwyn Garden City, with the residents housed at a maximum density of 12 units per acre.[97] As with Letchworth, there were significant problems in raising the necessary financial capital. This was partly due to the onset of an economic recession, but financial institutions were generally reluctant to fund a limited dividend company. After the establishment of Welwyn Garden City Ltd, Louis de Soissons (1890–1962) was appointed as architect and town planner.[98] He was a native of Canada who had come to England as a child, and eventually trained in the classical tradition at the Royal Academy Schools and the Ecole de Beaux Arts in Paris.[99] His involvement in the creation of Welwyn Garden City lasted for more than 40 years. As a designer, de Soissons was primarily responsible for giving a distinctive neo-Georgian character to the central area and much of the housing stock.

The rate of progress was very slow in the early years, to the point where the financial viability of the entire project was threatened. A major constraint on the growth of Welwyn Garden City was the lack of public support for infrastructure costs. At the start of 1922, only 260 houses were either completed or under construction, and only 1,000 residents were living within the official boundaries of the new settlement.[100] The few industrial firms in operation were subsidiaries of Welwyn Garden City Ltd. In 1924 the situation improved somewhat

ABOVE: Frederic J Osborn in his back garden at Welwyn Garden City. (Town & Country Planning Association)

93. Maurice de Soissons, *Welwyn Garden City: A Town Designed for Healthy Living* (Cambridge, 1988), p. 35.
94. Hardy, *From Garden Cities to New Towns*, p. 151.
95. M. de Soissons, *Welwyn Garden City*, p. 36.
96. Ibid.
97. Ibid., p. 40.
98. Ibid., p. 42
99. Ibid.
100. M. de Soissons, *Welwyn Garden City*, p. 51.

ABOVE: Aerial view of Welwyn Garden City.

RIGHT: 'Neo-Georgian' housing in Valley Road, Welwyn Garden City.

when two organisations with international reputations – Dawnay and Company (steel fabricators and construction engineers) and the American manufacturers of Shredded Wheat – decided to establish

ABOVE: Attractive group of terraced houses, Welwyn Garden City. (Town & Country Planning Association)

new premises at Welwyn Garden City.

By the start of the 1930s, over 2,000 houses had been completed along with 6 churches and 9 schools.[101] The number of businesses in operation had grown to 45 and more than 8,500 residents made their homes in the second garden city.[102] As the economic situation became more problematic, Howard's cherished principle of a limited dividend on share capital was abandoned in the hope of attracting new investors.[103] Although the industrial base expanded somewhat at Welwyn Garden City during the late 1930s, on the eve of WW2 the total population was still only one-third of the original target figure.[104]

101. Ibid., p. 75.
102. Ibid., p. 75.
103. Ibid., p. 81.
104. Ibid., p. 233.

LEGACY OF THE INTER-WAR DECADES

From a garden city perspective, the inter-war years were generally regarded as a time of missed opportunities and limited achievements. Although Welwyn Garden City had been launched in 1920, there were few signs of a national commitment to develop a network of new self-contained settlements across the whole of Britain. For the most part, central government policy had failed to produce a more integrated approach to housing and town planning reform. In the face of popular demands for better housing, the need for broader consideration of town planning principles was often ignored. New housing developments were commonly approved with little regard for the location of industry and, given the lack of effective controls on the growth patterns for major cities, urban sprawl continued apace.

The Garden Cities and Town Planning Association adapted its campaigning agenda to the economic realities of the inter-war decades. During the 1920s and 1930s, the industrial sectors of the British economy were in transition. Two years after the Armistice the economy slipped into recession. Despite a modest recovery in the late 1920s, the situation deteriorated dramatically during the 1930s in the face of global depression. In highly competitive conditions, Britain's traditional industries were failing to attract fresh capital for the modernisation of production methods.

As the traditional industries struggled to compete in world markets, new firms emerged to produce a range of innovative products such as motor cars, aircraft, canned foods, furniture, electrical goods and other home appliances. The growth pattern for these 'light' industries was highly uneven in geographic terms. The decline in traditional manufacturing was particularly acute in the Midlands, North of England and Scotland, however, these parts of the country failed to attract a reasonable share of the new industrial firms. In effect this was the beginning of what has come to be called the 'North-South Divide', with new industries locating mainly in the southeast of England along the major arterials serving the suburbs of Greater London.[105]

The pace and scale of suburbanisation during the inter-war decades were unprecedented. An extensive ring of low density housing was built around London, with piecemeal ribbon development stretching outward along the main roads. Without effective controls on the pattern of urban growth, complaints were frequently voiced about the undesirable impacts of urban sprawl on older settlements and open countryside. Between 1919 and 1939, the total population of Greater London increased by one-third, from 6 to 8 million. Rapid suburban development was made possible by extensions to the electric railway network and the London Underground. Over the period, the development footprint of

105. Hardy, *From Garden Cities to New Towns*, p. 191.

ABOVE: Promotional poster for Welwyn Garden City. (Town & Country Planning Association)

Greater London increased by a factor of 5.[106]

Suburban sprawl was by no means restricted to Greater London. Between 1919 and 1939, nearly 4 million new homes were constructed in England and Wales. Of the total number, 90 per cent were built in suburban locations. The tenure characteristics of these newly built houses were also novel. Two types of housing tenure expanded significantly during the period, rental accommodation provided directly by local authorities and individual owner-occupation.

In the immediate aftermath of WW1, local authority housebuilding was regarded as essential to remove the existing shortages. For the first 5 post-war years, local authorities accounted for about 60 per cent of all new residential construction in England and Wales.[107] When the financial provisions of the Housing and Town Planning Act of 1919 were withdrawn in 1921, housing shortages were still evident in many parts of the country. The policy of building additional working class housing for general needs was therefore extended under the Housing Acts of 1923 and 1924, which remained in force in England and Wales until 1929. Although the standards were somewhat less generous than those required under the 1919 Act, the promotion of low density, garden city style housing for families was still the overriding priority.

By 1930 the signs of severe housing shortages were much less evident around the country, and the costs of residential construction had fallen back to pre-1914 levels. In these conditions, a shift in the priorities of national housing policy was deemed to be necessary. Private developers were now seen to be in a more favourable position to provide modest forms of general needs housing for skilled working class families on a purely commercial basis. This would allow local authorities to redirect their housebuilding activities towards the relief of overcrowding and the removal of slum conditions.

In England and Wales, private sector housebuilding experienced a dramatic revival during the 1930s, with more than three-quarters of all new construction undertaken by private developers without any form of financial assistance.[108] A large share of these new homes were built to meet the growing demand for owner-occupation in suburban areas. This increase in home-ownership occurred at a time when the general economy was performing poorly. It was made possible by major innovations in the building society industry, which enabled new mortgages to be provided with longer repayment periods and lower regular payments.

106. Ibid., p. 171.

107. G. D. H. Cole, *Building and Planning* (London, 1945), Table 1, p. 91.

108. Ibid.

Many of the new suburban estates – in both the public and private sectors – were built without proper attention to the need for local services and community facilities. As noted previously, private housbuilders often advertised their new developments as garden city estates when in fact the detached bungalows and semi-detached units on offer were clearly out of favour with garden city supporters since they offered little scope for imaginative forms of grouping along street frontages.

Ironically, the garden city movement was frequently blamed for the negative repercussions of suburban development. One outspoken critic, Thomas Sharp, raised a number of fundamental questions about Howard's vision. Although Sharp recognised the need for new self-contained settlements, he strongly opposed the idea of trying to combine the theoretical advantages of town and country. As an ardent admirer of English town-building practice during the 17th, 18th and early 19th centuries, Sharp argued for policies aimed at retaining a clear distinction between town and countryside. He was also highly critical of new developments that attempted to recapture the feel of traditional English villages.

109. Hardy, *From Garden Cities to New Towns*, p. 213.

Although Ebenezer Howard remained sceptical about the potential benefits of state intervention, many of his followers came to a different view in the 1930s.[109] From the experience in promoting Letchworth and Welwyn Garden City, it had become apparent that the pace of development had been hampered from the outset by the lack of financial capital and public support for essential infrastructure. Major investment in infrastructure was needed at an early stage both to attract industry and to facilitate the provision of housing and related services. In financial terms, the need to fund infrastructure created a 'front loading problem' at a time when the sponsor's revenue stream was very limited. Without financial assistance from central or local government to support the early phases of development, the longer-term viability of the project was seriously threatened.

As economic depression came to characterise the 1930s, policy debates focused upon the urgent need for national planning. Given the general deterioration of the economy and the uneven pattern of new industrial development, there was a growing realisation that a regional planning approach was unlikely to be effective unless it was well co-ordinated within an overall national strategy which took account of key inter-regional factors. The Garden Cities and Town Planning

Association responded to this emerging debate, mainly by relating its traditional concerns more directly to questions of industrial policy and national planning.[110]

Frederic Osborn was instrumental in this transition. In 1936, after working for many years in various capacities at Letchworth and Welwyn Garden City, Osborn agreed to take on the role of Honorary Secretary of the Garden Cities and Town Planning Association.[111] As both a skilled campaigner, and a perceptive observer of political and economic affairs, he saw the potential for arguing the case for garden cities within the context of a national strategy for public control over industrial location. A year later, the Royal Commission on the Geographical Location of the Industrial Population was appointed under the chairmanship of Sir Montague Barlow, and Osborn recast the case for new self-contained settlements in the evidence given on behalf of the Garden Cities and Town Planning Association.[112] His submission to the Barlow Commission began by tracing the origins of the garden city idea and the lessons learned from the previous attempts to implement Howard's vision. He then documented the continuing causes of centralisation, the manifest problems resulting from uncontrolled development, and the shortcomings of the existing statutory framework for town and country planning. Based on this highly perceptive assessment of the current situation, Osborn offered a variety of suggestions concerning the desired direction of policies dealing with national planning, new town development, urban regeneration, statutory physical planning, building byelaws, housing administration, and the future of Greater London.

Under Frederic Osborn's stewardship, the image of the Garden Cities and Town Planning Association was transformed along with a basic change in attitude toward the potential benefits of state intervention. During WW2, Osborn worked tirelessly to influence official thinking on post-war reconstruction and many of his ideas were later incorporated in the legislation for the post-war British New Towns programme. In 1943, the Garden Cities and Town Planning Association changed its name to the Town and Country Planning Association, reputedly to acknowledge the vital contribution of the countryside and its people to the war effort. With this change in name, it became increasingly difficult for the general public to appreciate the original connection with Ebenezer Howard's vision. For the next 35 years, the spirit of the early garden city movement endured through the continuing commitment

110. Ibid., p. 190.
111. Ibid., p. 195.
112. Frederic J. Osborn, *Evidence of the Garden Cities and Town Planning Association Given to the Barlow Royal Commission on the Geographic Distribution of the Industrial Population* (London, 1938).

of Frederic Osborn who remained actively involved, virtually until his death in 1978 at the age of ninety-three.

3 Scottish Dimension of the Garden City Movement

GARDEN · CITY · ASSOCIATION.
West of Scotland Branch.

414, Sauchiehall Street.

MR. EBENEZER HOWARD

Will deliver a Lecture (illustrated
by Lime-light)

IN ATHENÆUM HALL,

On Thursday, Nov. 5, at 8 p.m.,
On

" LETCHWORTH—THE FIRST GARDEN CITY

And Its Development."

Sir John Ure Primrose, Bart.,
In the chair.

Admission : Stalls and Balcony, 2s.; Area and
Gallery, 1s.   Doors open at 7.30 p.m.   Tickets
to be had at the Athenæum.

PREVIOUS PAGE: Announcement of 1908 lecture by Ebenezer Howard, hosted by the Glasgow & West of Scotland Branch of the Garden City Association.

BELOW: Outline proposal for new garden suburb in the Gorgie area of Edinburgh, put forward by the Edinburgh & East of Scotland Branch of the Garden City Association.' (Reproduced with the permission of the National Library of Scotland.)

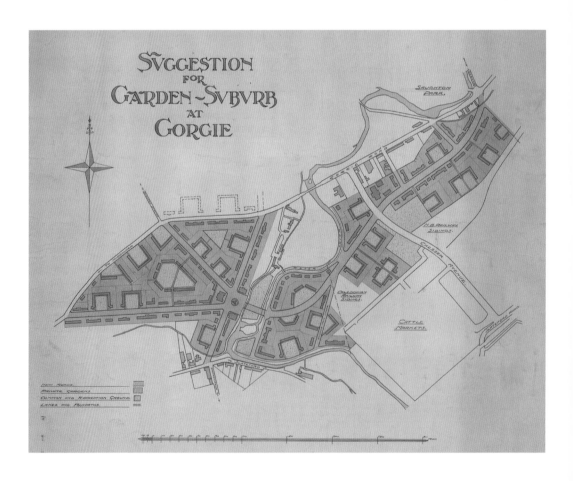

The overview of the Scottish experience presented in the remainder of this book has been pieced together from a variety of sources. In addition to reviewing the findings of recent research, a major effort was made to identify relevant information in the journals, official reports, and press coverage of the period. The magazine of the Garden City Association, initially titled *The Garden City*, was particularly useful in clarifying the chronology of events north of the Border. Two other methods were used in identifying and documenting specific developments of interest – systematic analysis of Valuation Roll data and site visits to collect visual material and gain a first-hand impression of the current state of the housing.

CONTRASTING OUTLOOKS IN ENGLAND AND SCOTLAND

In England during 1912 there was a general sense of optimism about the recent achievements of the garden city movement and the prospects for further progress. Henry Vivian, the driving force behind the promotion of co-partnership housing, commented on the current situation in *The Quarterly Review* as follows:

> Few movements in this country have taken such a hold on public opinion in so short a time as that in favour of better Housing and Town-planning. It is not many years ago that we had a few

voices crying in the wilderness; and these were regarded by the so-called practical man as Utopians and dreamers. The ideal of the average man in regard to housing our working town population did not soar beyond the building of huge blocks of tenements, one of the most hideous devices for rearing human beings that ingenuity could suggest. Wealthy men who genuinely believed themselves to be public benefactors, and 'progressive' public bodies, spent huge sums in our great cities in the erection of these monstrosities. In less than twenty years, opinion on this as well as other aspects of the question has been quite transformed by the new movement. The imagination has been stimulated, and a science of town development is gradually taking the place of the happy-go-lucky methods of previous generations. The time has, in fact, come when, on this question, we have to insist that, in the interest of race-preservation, private gain must harmonise with the public good.[1]

Around the same time, the prospects for embracing garden city ideas in Scotland seemed rather more pessimistic. This was partly due to the enduring legacy of the tenement tradition, which served to constrain the possibilities for lower density forms of development in and around the larger towns and cities. This predicament was discussed by James F. Roxburgh in an article that appeared in *The Blue Blanket – An Edinburgh Civic Review*:

> It cannot have escaped even the most casual observer of the Garden City and Town-Planning movement that hardly any progress has been made in Scotland. Garden Cities, Garden Suburbs, and Garden Villages are growing up everywhere in England, while in Scotland there is little or nothing to show. At the recent Town-Planning Conference held in Glasgow, it was almost pathetic to hear speaker after speaker assert that Garden Cities were impossible in Scotland on account of the high price of land, and that for the housing, at least of the artisan class, nothing but buildings of the present tenement type were possible. This statement is a complete inversion of the facts of the case. It is not the high price of land which makes tenements necessary. It is the prevalence of the tenement type of dwelling which inflates the price of land.[2]

1. Henry Vivian, 'Garden cities, housing and town-planning', *The Quarterly Review*, 1912, Vol. 216, No. 431, p. 493.
2. James F. Roxburgh, 'Town-planning in Scotland: the tenement problem', *The Blue Blanket – An Edinburgh Civic Review*, No. 4, October 1912, p. 316.

James Roxburgh was a solicitor who played a leading role in the formation of the Edinburgh & East of Scotland Branch of the Garden City Association. He was well aware of the difficulties that would need to be overcome in any concerted effort to bring about an end to tenement building in Scotland. Although strongly in favour of cottage provision for working class sections of the population, Roxburgh argued that in the prevailing circumstances it would be more realistic to focus on the need for a reformed approach to the design of traditional tenements:

> The 2-storey house must always be looked upon as the ideal dwelling. In a country like Scotland, however, with a tradition of tenements, we cannot expect all at once to get away from that type of building, and tenements in a modified form will, for a time at least, have a place in our Town Plans. In some areas where it is impossible to build cottages, we must arrange for tenements so modified as to get rid of the present defects.[3]

3. Ibid., pp. 320-1.

The Blue Blanket was a short-lived journal produced by the Edinburgh circle of Patrick Geddes, who was himself a committed supporter of the garden city movement. Roxburgh's views on the 'cottages versus tenements' question were recorded following a number of heated discussions at a series of annual conferences held in Scotland to promote the preparation of town planning schemes under the provisions of the Housing and Town Planning Act of 1909. The enabling powers for the preparation of town planning schemes applied specifically to the development of greenfield land on the periphery of larger cities and towns, and it was in this context that a lively public debate on the future of tenement construction emerged in Scotland.

At the time when Roxburgh's article was first published, it would have been difficult to predict the extent to which garden city ideas might exert an influence in Scotland during the years ahead. Both the impending responses to wartime conditions and the subsequent development of British housing policy could not have been foreseen in 1912.

CREATION OF GARDEN CITY ASSOCIATION
BRANCHES IN SCOTLAND

In the July 1906 issue of *The Garden City* an article appeared about the recent efforts of the Garden City Association to promote local and regional branches throughout Great Britain.[4] It was reported that in Scotland, Thomas Adams, the Honorary Secretary, had organised a series of lectures and meetings during the previous year in Aberdeen, Alexandria, Dundee, Glasgow, Edinburgh and Kirkintilloch. These gatherings provided an opportunity to update interested Scots on the latest developments at Letchworth and the aims of the Cheap Cottages Exhibition.

From a London perspective, there was also seen to be a growing need for the Garden City Association to have an organisational presence in Scotland given the recent decision taken by the Board of Admiralty to expand the naval base at Rosyth. This expansion would eventually require a significant amount of permanent accommodation for the workforce at Rosyth, which the Association regarded as a major opportunity for a new self-contained development based on garden city principles. With this objective in mind, preliminary discussions had taken place in London between representatives of the Association and senior Admiralty staff. Although these discussions were highly tentative, it was clear that there were a number of technical issues that could only be resolved in consultation with agencies operating on the ground in Scotland.

During the closing months of 1905, meetings were held in Edinburgh and Glasgow to promote the creation of separate branches of the Garden City Association. From the available information, it was not possible to determine the actual dates when the two branches were established. From the reporting of regional events in *The Garden City*, it is evident that the Edinburgh & East of Scotland Branch was organising various activities during 1908 and the Glasgow & West of Scotland Branch was similarly involved by the beginning of 1909. Both of these branches remained in operation until the outbreak of WW1. In all likelihood, both branches suspended activities for the duration of the war, and never regained their earlier momentum. A single Scottish Branch of the Garden Cities and Town Planning Association was formed in 1937 to address what were then seen as the most pressing issues in Scotland (see Chapter 7).[5]

4. *The Garden City*, New Series, Vol. I, No. 6, July 1906, p. 136.

5. *Town and Country Planning*, Vol. VI, No. 22, January 1938, p. 20.

Although the garden city movement was generally committed to the revitalisation of rural areas, neither the Edinburgh & East of Scotland Branch nor the Glasgow & West of Scotland Branch managed to play a significant part in the attempts to achieve land reform.[6] Both branches tended to maintain an urban orientation, although some attention was given to promoting small holdings in suburban locations and to improving the housing conditions of miners based at collieries near to larger settlements.

EDINBURGH & EAST OF SCOTLAND BRANCH

The main organisers of the Edinburgh & East of Scotland Branch were the aforementioned James F. Roxburgh and his law partner George Henderson. Roxburgh also served on the Council of the Garden City Association, which operated from a London base. Other leading figures within the branch included Richard Lodge, Professor of History at the University of Edinburgh and a founder of the Edinburgh University Settlement; Henry M. Cadell, a reform-minded landowner and noted geologist based in Bo'ness; Alexander Lorne Campbell, an Edinburgh architect; Helen L. Kerr, a follower of Octavia Hill who played a major part in the work of the Edinburgh Social Union; and Thomas B. Whitson, an accountant who had a long association with Patrick Geddes's civic improvement efforts within the medieval quarter of the city. A link with Edinburgh Town Council was maintained through the involvement of Councillor G. Malcolm Stewart who was keen to promote co-partnership initiatives in housing.

At the outset, the work of the Edinburgh & East of Scotland Branch was particularly concerned with the future development of Rosyth in Fife. Outline proposals for an ambitious garden city style development were initially prepared for the consideration of the Admiralty. However, neither this broad plan nor a more limited range of suggestions about permanent forms of housing were ever accepted by the Admiralty and the activists within the branch began to focus on other issues.

In order to raise awareness of the general aims and achievements of the wider garden city movement, the branch decided to participate in the Scottish National Exhibition of 1908 which was held at Edinburgh's

ABOVE: Publicity stamp promoting the 1908 Scottish National Exhibition held in Edinburgh.

BELOW: Premiated design by Ramsay Traquair for six miners cottages to be built near Stirling, at Bannockburn, under the auspices of the Edinburgh & East of Scotland Branch of the Garden City Association.

Saughton Park. An exhibit was mounted for this event in collaboration with First Garden City Ltd, the company responsible for the development of Letchworth. A large scale model of the general layout of Letchworth was the central feature of the display. Visitors were able to walk along a viewing platform in order to observe how the houses, factories, and other buildings had been positioned on the site without destroying the rural character of the area.[7]

Also during 1908 the branch sponsored a design competition for a small group of miners' cottages on a suitable site at Bannockburn in Stirlingshire. The site in question was owned by Mr and Mrs Steel-Maitland of Sauchieburn, who agreed that the winning entry would be built in that location with funds subscribed by themselves and several members of the branch executive.[8] The design submitted by Ramsay Traquair was awarded first place in the competition. This development involving a modest yet artistic group of 6 adjoining single-storey cottages with parlour, bedroom, good-sized kitchen, small scullery and bath was completed and occupied by May 1909.[9] The properties remained in use until the mid-1960s when the general area was redeveloped by the local authority.

Once the 1909 Housing and Town Planning Act of 1909 had received parliamentary approval, the branch attempted to promote a planned garden suburb on the south-western edge of Edinburgh. This proposal was intended to serve as a model for the development of large greenfield sites on the periphery of the city. It was also envisaged as a way of demonstrating the desirability of providing lower density cottages in the garden city style as an alternative to traditional Scottish

tenements. A memorial was presented to Edinburgh Town Council in 1910 suggesting a joint initiative in the Gorgie area on a large open site that was already in local authority ownership. Although this suggestion never came to fruition in the form proposed, the site was eventually used after WW1 to build two important local authority developments, known as Chesser and Hutchison, under the provisions of the Housing and Town Planning Act of 1919.

GLASGOW & WEST OF SCOTLAND BRANCH

The activities of the Glasgow & West of Scotland Branch were strongly linked to the arts and crafts movement, through the involvement of Robert Maclaurin who also played a key role in the work of the Scottish Guild of Handicraft.[10] In addition to Maclaurin several prominent politicians played significant parts in establishing the branch, including two former Lord Provosts of Glasgow – Sir Samuel Chisholm and Sir John Ure Primrose – and a former Conservative Member of Parliament Sir John Stirling-Maxwell.

The Glasgow & West of Scotland Branch initially sponsored an architectural competition that was intended to generate fresh ideas for the design of working class cottages. A public exhibition was held to display the winning entries, from 27th January to 28th February 1909.[11] The panel of judges included a number of well-known Glasgow architects, such as Charles Rennie Mackintosh and James Salmon.[12] Approximately 100 sets of plans and drawings were on public view in the Sauchiehall Street premises that were shared with the Scottish Guild of Handicraft.

The public exhibition was officially opened by Sir John Ure Primrose, who explained to those in attendance that the key objective of the competition was to promote low density cottages rather than the traditional form of tenement flats. In his speech, he expressed the personal view that:

It would be a happy day for Glasgow when such dwellings were erected, affording a maximum of sunlight and a free current of air around every window without contamination from a stagnant

6. For an account of the land settlement movement in Scotland after WW1, see Leah Leneman, *Fit for Heroes?* (Aberdeen, 1989).
7. *Garden Cities and Town Planning*, New Series, Vol. III, No. 30, September 1908, p. 128.
8. *Garden Cities and Town Planning*, New Series, Vol. III, No. 29, August 1908, pp. 107-8.
9. Ibid.
10. Elizabeth Cumming, *Hand, Heart and Soul* (Edinburgh, 2006), pp. 174-7.
11. *Garden Cities and Town Planning*, New Series, Vol. IV, No. 33, May 1909, pp. 189-93.
12. Ibid.

court behind. If our city could be more spread out, in the separate dwelling, you would make the family life more desirable, more self-contained, and more attractive in every respect.[13]

Robert Maclaurin wrote a lengthy review of the exhibition for a 'special garden city' issue of *The Scottish Architect*.[14] In this article, after congratulating the various recipients of awards, he went on to compare the relative costs of cottage and tenement construction and to indicate that before long he hoped the branch would be in a position to sponsor a new self-contained development along garden city lines.

In the years that followed, several of the leading members of the Glasgow & West of Scotland Branch did manage to play important roles in creating garden city style housing developments on a co-partnership basis. Robert Maclaurin was the driving force behind a small initiative called Stirling Homesteads that was completed in 1910.[15] Two years later, Sir John Stirling-Maxwell successfully promoted the development of Westerton Garden Suburb on a site near Bearsden (see Chapter 4).[16]

RELATIONS WITH THE MAINSTREAM GARDEN CITY MOVEMENT

The two branches in Scotland were supported in various ways by the parent body in London. In September 1908 Ewart G. Culpin, the Secretary of the Garden City Association, travelled to Fife in order to observe and discuss the current situation at Rosyth.[17] During the following month, Ebenezer Howard made a lecture tour that included public meetings in Dundee, Dunfermline, Edinburgh, Glasgow, Greenock, Hamilton, Paisley, Port Glasgow, Stirling, and Uddingston.[18] Although some of these gatherings were not well attended, Howard's personal appearances did help to raise the profile of the garden city movement in Scotland. At the Port Glasgow meeting, he chatted with a group of young workers based in the Greenock area who were keen to live in cottages overlooking the River Clyde.[19] Inspired by this exchange of ideas, the group of workers eventually managed to promote a small development of co-partnership housing above Gourock, which is discussed further in Chapter 4.

A number of unsuccessful proposals for ambitious garden city

13. *Garden Cities and Town Planning*, New Series, Vol. IV, No. 33, May 1909, pp. 189-93.
14. Ibid.
15. Peter Aitken, Cameron Cunningham and Bob McCutcheon, *Notes for a New History of Stirling: The Homesteads, Stirling's Garden Suburb* (Stirling, 1984), p. 27.
16. *Garden Cities and Town Planning*, New Series, Vol. II, No. 11, November 1912.
17. *Garden Cities and Town Planning*, New Series, Vol. III, No. 31, December 1908, p. 152.
18. *Garden Cities and Town Planning*, New Series, Vol. III, No. 30, September 1908, p. 133.
19. *Garden Cities and Town Planning*, New Series, Vol. IV, No. 32, January–February 1909, p. 166.

developments were promoted for Scottish locations at various times. In some instances the sponsors were based in Scotland, but in other cases the proposals came from supporters of the mainstream garden city movement in London. In 1911 the Glasgow & West of Scotland Branch was associated with a proposal put forward by John Peacock for a new garden suburb at Clydebank.[20] An initial meeting to discuss this venture appeared promising, but significant difficulties soon arose when Peacock tried to raise the required capital. Apparently a site on the edge of Clydebank was acquired and a few cottages were actually built, however, the overall plan for a new garden suburb was eventually abandoned due to lack of funds.[21]

At least two additional proposals called for the development of a full-scale garden city in Scotland. During the closing stages of WW1 Captain George Swinton, then Chairman of London County Council and a former officer of the Highland Light Infantry, promoted the idea that a new self-contained garden city in the West of Scotland should be linked to the construction of a Forth and Clyde Ship Canal for ocean-going vessels.[22] This suggestion was discussed at a special meeting of the Garden Cities and Town Planning Association held in London at the start of 1918. Within government circles, a ship canal connecting the Forth and Clyde estuaries had been under consideration for several decades, as a means of advancing British naval and commercial interests. The feasibility of the ship canal was seriously questioned on cost-effectiveness grounds, and the general concept was eventually abandoned along with any notional ideas about the future development of a linked garden city.

Some years later, in 1925, a group based in the West of Scotland issued a prospectus for the establishment of Third Garden City Ltd, a new company that was to be formed for the purpose of developing a satellite town for Glasgow near the banks of Loch Lomond.[23] For a time, the sponsors attempted to increase public awareness of the need for more effective and imaginative town planning in Scotland. The proposal for a third (British) garden city, however, was eventually withdrawn due to the disappointing level of response from potential investors.

20. *Garden Cities and Town Planning*, New Series, Vol. I, No. 4, May 1911, p. 50.
21. Ewart G. Culpin, *The garden city movement Up-to-Date* (London, 1913), p. 26.
22. *Garden Cities and Town Planning*, New Series, Vol. VIII, No. 2, May 1918, pp. 36-7.
23. *Garden Cities and Town Planning*, New Series, Vol. 15, No. 8, August 1925, pp. 185 & 207.

MOUNTING DEBATE ABOUT COTTAGES VERSUS TENEMENTS

As noted earlier, the passage of the Housing and Town Planning Act of 1909 was in effect responsible for stimulating a major debate in Scotland about banning tenement construction altogether, reforming the design of newly-built tenements, and promoting the development of lower density forms of working class housing. Members of the two branches of the Garden City Association were active participants in the ensuing debate.

The new enabling powers of the 1909 Act included provisions for the preparation of town planning schemes for large tracts of undeveloped land on the periphery of major towns and cities. In preparing such schemes, it was necessary to determine the types of residential construction that would be permitted within the given sites. At this time there were still no subsidies available from central government to help cover the costs of housebuilding, regardless of whether the accommodation was intended to meet general needs or to rehouse those displaced by slum clearance initiatives.

In the absence of subsidies, much of the debate focused on the economic feasibility of providing modest cottages for skilled working class families in suburban locations on a purely commercial basis. Not surprisingly, the high cost of land in urban Scotland was seen to be a serious constraint, although opinions varied on this issue. Some observers argued that if effective measures were taken to restrict the density of development to a level that required cottage building, land prices would adjust downward to facilitate the desired type of development. Others were less convinced that local authorities would be able to impose the necessary regulations on housing density.

In 1911 the Local Government Board for Scotland and the National Housing and Town Planning Council organised the first of a series of annual conferences to promote the preparation of town planning schemes. These conferences were 2-day events, attended mainly by local authority elected members and senior officers along with public health professionals, housing reformers, and practicing architects. The first conference was held in Edinburgh at the end of March 1911. Thereafter, the venue of the annual conference alternated between Glasgow and Edinburgh.

For nearly a decade, the mainstream Garden City Association had been working closely with the National Housing and Town Planning Council, whose leading figures were Alderman William Thompson of Richmond Borough and Henry R. Aldridge. At the initial conference in Edinburgh, a Scottish Committee of the National Housing and Town Planning Council was formed with a remit to organise a series of annual conferences on this theme. The work of the Scottish Committee was co-ordinated by William E. Whyte, a senior official of the District Committee of the Middle Ward of Lanark County.

This series of annual conferences was eventually interrupted by the war. Until then the sessions were generally well attended and widely publicised in the Scottish press. A number of speakers at the first conference reported on the recent progress of the garden city movement which focused attention on the artisan quarters built at Letchworth and Hampstead Garden Suburb. For the most part, the delegates accepted that single-family cottages with private gardens would be preferable to traditional tenements from the standpoints of public health, personal hygiene, general amenity and wholesome family life. The tenement system was roundly criticised, but very few of the delegates were convinced that well-designed artisan cottages could be produced in Scotland at affordable rents. The Burgh Surveyor of Govan, for example, felt that it was unrealistic to presume that tenement construction could be ended in the near future, and he therefore advised that greater attention should be given to reforming the design of traditional Scottish tenements.[24]

24. *Glasgow Herald*, 20 June 1912, p. 12. 25. Philip Mairet, *Pioneer of Sociology* (London, 1957), p. 139.

PATRICK GEDDES AND THE TENEMENT QUESTION

The Scottish polymath Patrick Geddes (1854–1932) is generally regarded as one of the pioneers of modern town planning. Although proud of his Scottish heritage, Geddes was appalled by the slum conditions that persisted in many parts of the country. During the 1880s and 1890s, he was directly involved in improving living conditions in Edinburgh's Old Town, the medieval quarter of the city. Within this historic urban fabric, Geddes was strongly opposed to the idea of large-scale demolition. In this context, he favoured an alternative approach which in his later writings was called 'conservative surgery'.

ABOVE: Scottish polymath Patrick Geddes.

This unorthodox style of gradual renewal was in his view preferable to comprehensive redevelopment on several grounds. He considered it to be a more sensitive approach to the physical upgrading of the historic built environment as well as a more humane way of meeting the needs of impoverished local residents. In addition, he argued that conservative surgery was a more cost-effective solution than comprehensive redevelopment.

In his efforts to improve living conditions in the Old Town, Geddes tried to combine an imaginative mix of rehabilitation and radical reconstruction of older buildings with a limited amount of infill new building on gap sites. Where a limited amount of demolition was seen to be justified, it was important for any infill new construction to respect the scale and character of the older surviving buildings. Geddes's views about the desired pattern of growth for Scottish cities are less well known than his preferred approach for the regeneration of older urban areas. As we have seen, the earliest forms of traditional Scottish tenements evolved within the medieval quarter of Edinburgh. When Geddes was co-ordinating his improvement projects in the Lawnmarket area, he generally respected the tenements that were constructed over the centuries. In view of this, it is often assumed that he was a strong proponent of tenement living. Geddes was in fact highly critical of the tenement system and a committed supporter of the garden city movement. He firmly opposed the construction of new tenements in suburban locations, and was keen to ensure that residential development on the periphery of Scottish cities and towns took the form of well-planned low density cottages for a wide range of income groups.

Geddes recognised that Ebenezer Howard's vision for garden cities was consistent with his own views on the need for decentralisation, regional autonomy, devolved control over local affairs and the revitalisation of civic life through voluntary action.[25] Between 1903 and 1913, Geddes spent much of his time in London, trying to obtain support for worthwhile projects such as the reconstruction of Crosby Hall or participating in the work of the Cities Committee of the Sociological Society.[26] During this period, he contributed various articles to the monthly magazine of the Garden City Association and served as one of the organisation's many Honorary Vice Presidents. He also frequently took part in conferences and study tours. Although he was not directly involved in promoting either of the two branches in Scotland, he did try

25. Philip Mairet, *Pioneer of Sociology* (London, 1957), p. 139.
26. Helen Meller, *Patrick Geddes: Social Evolutionist and Town Planner* (London, 1990), pp. 138-9 & 148.

to support garden city ideas north of the Border. In 1905, for example, he hosted a visiting party of Scots who had travelled to Letchworth to take in the Cheap Cottages Exhibition.[27]

In his writings, Geddes often criticised the Scottish tenement tradition. The following passage from *Cities in Evolution*, his best known book, expresses his profound disenchantment with the impact of tenement conditions on Scottish life:

> There is no word which can convey to ordinary old fashioned English readers – who still cling to the national idea on which they were brought up, of homes as separate houses, of each family with its own bit of ground, at least its yard, however small – the full content and savour which our Scottish cities – Historic Edinburgh, Great Glasgow, Bonnie Dundee, and minor ones, with burghs without number – manage to condense and to express in their, in one sense, high tradition of 'Working-class Tenements'. Inspiring name! These are inhabited by the majority of the Scottish people: more than half the whole population in fact, are in one- and two-room tenements – a state of things unparalleled in Europe or America, in fact, in the history of civilisation.[28]

27. *The Garden City*, Vol. I, No. 5, November 1905, p. 86.
28. Patrick Geddes, *Cities in Evolution* (London, 1968), p. 134.

Geddes was also well aware that tenement living had become deeply engrained in Scottish culture. He recognised that various interests in Scottish society were benefiting financially from the perpetuation of tenement building. The shift to cottage provision on greenfield sites would not be easily achieved in the circumstances

> when ... some little Housing discussion is raised in Scotland, the tenements, and even their one- and two-roomed components, still find no lack of advocates, and these among all classes! Not only do individuals speak in their defence, but even local pride is aroused. The fact is, we rather look down upon small brick houses: we admire our lofty piles of stone: we still use their historic and legal name of 'Lands'. Finally, the whole matter is put upon what are really high metaphysical grounds ... We are made to feel a certain fitness in these things, a certain established harmony; in fact a sort of foreordination of Scotsmen for tenements, and of tenements for Scotsmen. Upon these towering

heights of national destiny, therefore the economic verdict is easy to give, and hard to refuse – that 'we can afford nothing better'. Economic explanations are added by some, and political explanations of these by others: none of them sufficient.[29]

The situation was especially problematic in Edinburgh, where much of the peripheral land was controlled by a consortium of charitable educational trusts accustomed to financing their schools from surpluses generated by tenement development. Geddes commented on the irony of this predicament in a paper given at the RIBA Town Planning Conference of 1910:

It is important to note how that essential continuance of the historic overcrowding of Edinburgh by the habitual preference of even moderately well-to-do and otherwise intelligent people for the tenement, as distinguished from the cottage, had been and still is encouraged by the great Educational Trusts, which are the largest ground landlords of Edinburgh, and which stoutly continue to press in and pile up a population far denser than that which can be found upon the estates of any of the ordinary types of ground landlords of whom English town-planners so often grievously complain – and yet all this with the best intentions, in the supposed interest of the up-bringing of the child-life of Edinburgh![30]

About a year earlier, Geddes participated in a study visit to Germany that was organised by the National Housing Reform Council. This tour gave him an opportunity to observe the results of some of the recent town extension plans for German cities, which had been generally praised by T. C. Horsfall in his 1904 publication titled *The Improvement of the Dwellings and Surroundings of the People: The Example of Germany.* On the basis of Horsfall's assessment, Geddes was expecting to see impressive examples of a planned transition from high density tenements to cottage provision. He was therefore shocked to find that in many of the places visited, the construction of multi-storey tenements was still occurring within the areas covered by town extension plans. These situations raised serious doubts in his mind about the achievements of the German planning system, and in *Cities in Evolution* he commented

29. Ibid., pp. 137-8.
30. Patrick Geddes, 'The civic survey of Edinburgh' in Royal Institute of British Architects, Transactions of Town Planning Conference – London, 10–15 October 1910, p. 566.

on the potential implications for future developments in Scotland:

> Learn from Germany? Certainly yes! Imitate Germany? Certainly
> no! With all her plannings, with all her commanding foresight,
> her public enterprise, it is still from Letchworth and Hampstead,
> from Woodlands and Earswick, and the like, as of course from
> the old-world villages they continue to renew, that we may best
> learn to house our people in moderate numbers to the acre, and
> with the most essential of conditions of health for children,
> wife and man alike – that is of cottage and garden. In Scotland,
> we forget this. The evil Continental tradition of walled cities
> and crowded population, and consequent persistence of high
> site values, still weighs heavily upon our long war-worn land...[31]

Geddes had a particular talent for synthesis and was generally willing to recognise and build upon the sound ideas of others. Although
deeply committed to the settling of international conflicts by peaceful
means, he welcomed the garden city style that was built in Scotland
for civilian defence workers during the course of WW1. The following
passage makes clear that he had few, if any, reservations about intro-
ducing what was commonly seen as an 'English' form of housing into
the Scottish landscape:

> How can we hope to bring in better housing among a people
> whose high and abstract cultivation thus lifts them above com-
> mon ground wherever they may go. We must fall back upon
> importing missionaries! Happily these sometimes desirable
> aliens have lately been forthcoming. Like honey from the carcase
> of a lion, a peaceful advance of industry and well-being may
> be gained from the very heart of war. Thus the transference of
> some hundreds of torpedo workers from Woolwich to the Clyde
> lately brought with it the needful discontent with tenement
> conditions, with disgust, refusal even; and a garden village for
> these soundest, wisest, and most successful of strike-leaders...
> is therefore already in progress.[32]

Geddes also had a special talent for combining theory and practice.
Although his best known practical initiatives in Scotland were under-

31. Ibid.
32. Cmd. 230, pp. xxxiii-xxxiv.

33. These properties were first listed in the Edinburgh Valuation Roll for Financial Year 1907–08.

taken within the Old Town of Edinburgh, during the early 1900s he also attempted to promote a suburban garden village in the Coltbridge area to the west of Haymarket. Unfortunately his original aims for this project were never realised, but he did manage to complete a terrace of 2-storey cottages at Nos. 1–7 Roseburn Cliff by the end of 1907.[33] These relatively modest cottages were designed in an arts and crafts manner by the local architectural firm of McArthy and Watson. Apparently the intention was to create an opportunity for affordable owner-occupation in a convenient and attractive inner-suburban location. The 7 cottages, which lie within the Coltbridge and Wester Coates Conservation Area, are now designated as Grade C Listed Buildings.

BALLANTYNE COMMISSION FINDINGS ON TENEMENT BUILDING

Pressures for an official investigation of Scottish housing conditions began to build up through the work of the Royal Commission on Mines, appointed in 1906 to look into the health and safety of miners. To a limited extent, the findings of this body drew attention to poor housing conditions in Scottish mining villages. In response to the

critical comments of the Royal Commission on the Mines, representatives of the Scottish Miners Federation requested the Secretary for
Scotland in 1909 to set up a formal inquiry into the housing conditions of mineworkers. The Local Government Board for Scotland was
then asked to instruct various Medical Officers of Health to prepare
reports on the conditions found in their respective areas. These
reports were published by the end of 1910. The findings highlighted
the need for a more comprehensive investigation of working class
housing conditions across the whole of Scotland and a Royal Commission was eventually appointed in October 1912, officially named
The Royal Commission on the Housing of the Industrial Population
of Scotland – Rural and Urban.

The 1912 Royal Commission on Housing was given a remit to in-
quire 'into the housing of the industrial population of Scotland, rural
and urban (with special reference in the rural districts to the housing
of miners and agricultural labourers), and to report what legislative or
administrative action is in their opinion desirable to remedy existing
defects'.[34] Sir Henry Ballantyne (1855–1941) was appointed to chair the
Royal Commission. Ballantyne was a Borders woollen mill owner and
Liberal Party activist, who had served as Provost of the Royal Burgh
of Peebles from 1898 to 1907. The other 11 members had diverse occu-
pational backgrounds and political affiliations. They were drawn from
various parts of Scotland.

The work of the Ballantyne Commission was undertaken over a 5-year
period. A total of 155 sittings were held in a number of different locations,
mainly for the purpose of receiving evidence from witnesses.[35] The first
sitting was held in March 1913 and the last took place in October 1915.[36]
All aspects of the investigation were suspended 4 months later on
account of the war. Official permission was given to resume the work
at the start of 1917.[37] The final report was completed and published by
the end of that year.

The report covered a wide range of themes relating to working class
housing conditions in Scotland. Among the key issues examined were
the advantages and disadvantages of the Scottish tenement system and
the relative costs of tenement and cottage construction. Although the
question of garden cities was not addressed directly, the Commissioners
did manage to explore the recent experience of public utility societies
and tenant co-partnership initiatives in England. Official visits were

34. Cd. 8731, Report of the
Royal Commission on the
Housing of the Industrial
Population of Scotland –
Rural and Urban (Edinburgh,
1917), p. 1.
35. Ibid.
36. Ibid.
37. Ibid.

ABOVE: Sir Henry Ballantyne,
Chairman of the 1912 Royal
Commission on Housing in
Scotland – Rural and Urban.
(Courtesy of the Local History
and Archive Service, Heritage
Hub, Heart of Hawick, Scottish
Borders Council).

undertaken to observe cottage developments at Bournville, Ealing, Hampstead Garden Suburb, Harborne, Letchworth, New Earswick, and the Woodlands estate for colliery workers in Doncaster.[38] Additional perspectives on the recent English experience were gained through the personal evidence given in Scotland by key figures such as Henry Aldridge, J. S. Nettlefold and Henry Vivian.

After due deliberation, the members of the Ballantyne Commission were not persuaded by the arguments to put an end to tenement construction. They opted instead for an approach aimed at reforming the design of tenements and controlling the density of development. The relevant recommendations were set out in the final report as follows:[39]

38. Cd. 8731, p. 3 and *Scotsman*, 16 February 1914, p. 2.
39. Cd. 8731, pp. 37-8.

No tenement should be more than 3 storeys (including the ground floor).

None of the houses entering off the common stair should be in the nature of back-to-back houses.

Tenements should be arranged in blocks as separate or detached pavilions, so as to admit a sufficiency of light and air.

There should be sufficient open space about tenements to provide adequately for ventilation, and sufficient space in the immediate neighbourhood to allow for children's playgrounds, public bowling greens and gardens, a certain number of private gardens to the houses, and so far as possible, a separate bleaching and drying green to each house.

No tenements should be allowed in the form of hollow squares.

Where tenements of 3 storeys are erected, not more than 32 houses per acre should be allowed.

Where double-flatted houses (4-in-a-block cottage flats) are erected, not more than 24 houses to the acre should be allowed.

Where single cottages are erected, not more than 16 cottages to the acre should be allowed (as compared with the Garden City maxima of 12 to the acre in urban areas and 8 to the acre in rural areas).

These recommendations were never formally included in the new Scottish legislation that received parliamentary approval in 1919. In a less formal way, they were subsequently used by the Local Government Board for Scotland as benchmarks for the developments built under the Housing and Town Planning (Scotland) Act of 1919.

The earliest garden city influences on the development of working class housing began to appear in Scotland during the years immediately prior to the outbreak of WW1, and were subsequently extended through the wartime efforts to provide cottage accommodation for incoming civilian defence workers.

4 New Forms of Cottage Provision in Scotland 1910–1914

PREVIOUS PAGE: Logo of Stirling Homesteads Ltd, sponsor of co-partnership development on the edge of Stirling. Courtesy of 'Collections of Stirling Smith Art Gallery and Museum'.

BELOW: Panorama of Falside Road development in Paisley, undertaken by public utility society formed by Brown & Polson. (Photo: J. Rosser)

Between 1910 and 1914, a small number of new cottage developments were built for the benefit of skilled working class families in Scotland. These developments were undertaken by a handful of progressive local authorities and voluntary bodies. In some instances, the sponsoring organisations were influenced by the English experience under the 1890 Housing of the Working Classes Act and by the early achievements of the mainstream garden city movement. This chapter provides more detailed information on the initial efforts in Scotland to promote working class cottage accommodation prior to the outbreak of WW1.

1. Cd. 8731, Report of the Royal Commission on the Housing of the Industrial Population of Scotland – Rural and Urban, p. 300.

SCOTTISH PATTERN OF LOCAL AUTHORITY HOUSEBUILDING

By 1914 local authorities in Scotland had managed to build a total of only 3,550 dwellings using the enabling powers of the 1890 Housing Act.[1] Glasgow and Edinburgh accounted for fully two-thirds of this figure. The bulk of the local authority completions were linked to slum clearance schemes carried out under Part 1 of the 1890 Act. By comparison, the Part 3 provisions for general needs housebuilding were seldom used in Scotland. The rehousing accommodation for those who were displaced by slum clearance schemes tended to be built within central rather than suburban locations. These local authority developments usually contained a preponderance of flats, especially deck access blocks designed with public health objectives in mind.

The shift towards local authority cottage building in Scotland, under Part 3 of the 1890 Act, was influenced by the research carried out during 1909 and 1910 by Medical Officers of Health into housing conditions of miners. One of these reports was prepared by the Medical Officer for Lanark County. Although in some parts of the country the Medical Officers' findings had produced positive responses from mine owners, there was little evidence of similar progress in Lanarkshire. The District Committee of the Middle Ward of Lanark County therefore decided in 1913 to use the Part 3 powers of the 1890 Act to develop cottage accommodation in several mining villages. A key figure in promoting this policy decision was William E. Whyte (1876–1950), the Clerk and Treasurer of the District Committee of Mid-Lanark, who for several years had been actively involved in the Scottish Committee of the National Housing and Town Planning Council.

2. Cd. 8041, Twentieth Annual Report of the Local Government Board for Scotland, 1914, p. lxx.

LOCAL AUTHORITY COTTAGE DEVELOPMENTS IN LANARKSHIRE

William Whyte managed to convince the Mid-Lanark District Committee that the stock of decent housing for miners should be expanded by direct building of attractive cottage accommodation for rent. In 1913, the District Committee decided to construct 50 cottages in the village of Cleland and 100 cottages in Harthill.[2] Both of these developments involved a mix of single-storey semi-detached units (with sitting room, bedroom, scullery, bathroom and larder) and 2-storey semi-detached properties (with sitting room, 2 or 3 bedrooms, scullery, bathroom, and larder).

Around the same time, the Burgh of Motherwell also decided to build a small development of 30 semi-detached cottages to the south of the town centre, in George Street and Broomside Street. Although it has not been possible to identify the full extent of local authority cottage building in the years immediately preceding the outbreak of WW1, these developments in Lanarkshire are particularly interesting examples of single-family cottages as distinct from cottage flats. Some examples of local authority cottage flats dating from this period can be found in Clydebank (Richmond Street, Whitecrook), Dumfries (Municipal Terrace, Brooms Road) and Glasgow (Royston Square,

LEFT: Local authority cottage development in Knowenoble Street, Cleland, Lanarkshire.

BELOW: View of Knowenoble Street, Cleland today. (Photo: J. Rosser)

RIGHT: Pre-WW1 local authority cottages in Broomside Street, Motherwell. (Photo: J. Rosser)

ABOVE: Sir William E. Whyte, prominent figure in the development of housing reform and modern town planning in Scotland. (Courtesy of the Archive Service, Glasgow Life, Mitchell Library, Glasgow).

formerly known as Garngad Square). As explained in the next chapter, Lanarkshire continued to play an important role in the provision of cottage accommodation for incoming civilian defence workers during the course of WW1.

Unfortunately, William Whyte has remained a somewhat neglected figure in the history of housing and town planning reform in Scotland. A native of Dumbarton, Whyte trained as a solicitor at Glasgow University. From his initial contributions in Lanarkshire, he went on to become an acknowledged expert on housing policy, town planning, and local government in Scotland through his numerous publications on these subjects. He continued in his role as Clerk and Treasurer of the Middle Ward of Lanark County until the reorganisation of Scottish local government in 1929. The following year he received a knighthood for services to local government. During the 1930s, his expertise was recognised beyond the boundaries of Scotland when he was appointed to serve on prestigious bodies such as the Marley Committee and the Barlow Commission on the Location of Industry. Sir William Whyte retained a lifelong interest in town planning and the garden city movement. Although neither an architect nor a town planner by profession, when a Scottish Branch of the Town Planning Institute was formally established in 1930, he was asked to preside at the initial meeting and agreed to serve as Honorary Chairman. Similarly, when a Scottish Branch of the Garden Cities and Town Planning Association was set up in 1937, he agreed to serve as President.

JOHN WHEATLEY'S CAMPAIGN FOR £8 COTTAGES

John Wheatley (1869–1930) was among the renowned group of Clydeside socialists elected to Parliament in 1922. He earned a national reputation as Minister of Health in the short-lived minority Labour government of 1924. During his brief period of service as a Cabinet minister, he sponsored the Housing (Financial Provisions) Act of 1924 which established the financial framework for the continuing subsidisation of housing construction for general needs across the whole of Great Britain. This legislation remained in force in England and Wales until 1929 and in Scotland until 1933. Over the years, the terms 'Wheatley Act of 1924' and 'Wheatley Act houses' have been commonly used in the literature as well as in everyday conversations within local communities.

At an earlier stage in his political career, Wheatley proposed an extensive programme of municipal cottage building in Glasgow as a newly elected member of the Town Council. He presented his ideas in a pamphlet titled *Eight Pound Cottages for Glasgow Citizens* which was published by the Glasgow Labour Party.[3] Towards the end of 1913, he gave evidence to the Ballantyne Commission which included an explanation of the underlying rationale for this proposal and the intended method of funding.

3. John Wheatley, *Eight Pound Cottages for Glasgow Citizens*, Glasgow Labour Party, 1913.
4. Ibid, p. 6.

Wheatley was persuaded by the arguments of public health reformers and felt that it was essential to put an end to tenement construction in Scotland. In practice, he recognised that a substantial amount of new working class housing would need to be built before the worst of the existing tenements could be demolished on any scale. He therefore proposed that Glasgow Corporation should directly construct a large number of cottages within the existing city boundaries and on outlying sites that were legally controlled by the surrounding local authorities. Capital funding for these new low density developments could be provided from the mounting surpluses of the municipal Tramway Department, in the form of non-interest-bearing loans.[4]

With the benefit of this source of finance, Wheatley argued that it would be feasible to develop terraced cottages with 3 bedrooms which could be occupied for an affordable rent that was equivalent to £8 *per annum*. This amount of rent was comparable to the current charge for a decent single-apartment flat in a working class Glasgow tenement. The proposed single-family cottages were to be built in 2-storey terraces of

5. Ibid., p. 8.
6. Ibid.

10 properties, at a density level of 15 units to the acre.[5] A garden area of
130 square yards was to be provided for each house.[6] The architectural
images shown in the pamphlet *Eight Pound Cottages for Glasgow Citizens*
do not suggest any direct influences of garden city design principles.
Although Wheatley's proposal was never adopted by Glasgow Corporation (Labour did not win majority control of the Council until the
mid-1930s), it did add fuel to the cottages versus tenements debate.

VOLUNTARY SECTOR DEVELOPMENTS IN SCOTLAND

In the years that immediately preceded WW1, a small number of registered public utility societies in Scotland were actively engaged in housebuilding on a non-profit or limited-profit basis. The final report of the Ballantyne Commission indicated that only 8 Scottish-based organisations were registered for housing purposes under the Industrial and Provident Societies Act. These bodies were eligible to obtain loan finance from the Public Works Loan Commissioners, subject to conditions defined in the Housing and Town Planning Act of 1909.[7] Although the Ballantyne Commission report did not identify the 8 organisations by name, the view was expressed that collectively their efforts had made 'almost no headway' in ameliorating the adverse housing conditions north of the Border.[8]

In researching this book, an effort was made to clarify the specific contributions of public utility societies in Scotland that had received loan finance under the provisions of the 1909 Act. These investigations revealed that between 1910 and 1914, 9 organisations had built a total of around 300 houses, mainly in West Central Scotland. As a rule the developments were relatively small in size. The majority involved fewer than 20 houses, and none of the developments exceeded 100 units. In several cases, larger numbers of properties were originally envisaged but the onset of the war resulted in the curtailment of construction activity. As will become apparent in the discussion below, there were some evident connections to both the garden city and tenant co-partnership movements.

WESTERTON GARDEN SUBURB

Westerton Garden Suburb is situated on the north-western edge of Glasgow. It is the largest and in many respects the most impressive example of garden city inspired development undertaken in Scotland prior to the outbreak of WW1. The project was sponsored by some of the prominent members of the Glasgow & West of Scotland Branch of the Garden City Association.

The initial stimulus for the project came from a meeting of the Glasgow & West of Scotland Branch held in December 1910.[9] On this

7. Cd. 8731, p. 269.
8. Ibid., pp. 269-70.
9. Maureen Whitelaw, *A Garden Suburb for Glasgow: The Story of Westerton* (Privately printed, 1992), pp. 5-9.

occasion, the featured speaker was Councillor T. R. Marr of Manchester, a native Scot and a close associate of Patrick Geddes. His talk entitled 'A Garden Suburb for Glasgow' was based on his recent experience in helping to create Burnage Garden Village on a tenant co-partnership basis in the Levenshulme area of Manchester.

This meeting was chaired by Sir John Stirling-Maxwell (1866–1956), a Tory politician with major interests in philanthropy and the arts, who had served from 1895 to 1906 as the Conservative Member of Parliament for the College Division of Glasgow. Marr's account of the Burnage experience was well received by the local supporters of the garden city movement, and a follow-up meeting was scheduled for the end of January 1911 to discuss the possibilities for a similar development in the suburbs of Glasgow. That meeting was also attended by Sir Hugh Shaw Stewart (1854–1942), another Tory politician who had sizeable holdings of land in the general vicinity of Greenock.[10] Shaw Stewart had served from 1886 to 1906 as the Conservative Member of Parliament for East Renfrewshire and was eventually to provide a site for one of the public utility society developments in the Greenock area discussed later in the chapter.

Under the stewardship of Sir John Stirling-Maxwell the development known as Westerton Garden Suburb gradually took shape over the next two years. After an extensive search for a suitable suburban location, a site was obtained in Canniesburn, on the Garscube estate of Sir Archibald Campbell of Succoth.[11] In August 1912, Glasgow Garden Suburb Tenants Ltd was formed as a co-partnership society and registered under the Industrial and Provident Societies Act.[12] Once an outline plan for the new development had been prepared, an application for loan finance was submitted to the Public Works Loan Commissioners. At this stage a minimum of 300 cottages was envisaged by the sponsors. To accommodate a community of this size, the landowner granted Glasgow Garden Suburb Ltd an option to acquire up to 200 acres of open land.

The Glasgow architectural practice of Grant and Gardner was appointed to design the desired range of accommodation, with Raymond Unwin acting as consultant on site layout. Design of the housing at Westerton Garden Suburb is usually attributed to John A. W. Grant, who went on to produce a number of other impressive garden city style developments in the years ahead (see Chapter 7). The variety of uses provided on the site is indicative of the potential advantages of

10. Ibid.
11. Ibid.
12. Ibid.

the tenant co-partnership approach. In addition to an attractive stock of single-family cottages with private gardens, the co-partnership society was able to include on the site a generous amount of common open space along with bowling greens, tennis courts, playgrounds for children and a village hall.[13]

From the outset, the intention was to cater for a range of income groups, with a large share of skilled working class households in relatively secure employment. The modest artisan cottages within the garden suburb were built to a standard not previously available in the Glasgow area. Many of the original residents were employed by the General Post Office. The location was initially very isolated, and there were problems in commuting to workplaces in central areas of the city. After protracted negotiations, however, the North British Railway Company agreed to provide a convenient new station on the Dumbarton and Helensburgh line.

In April 1913, the Committee of Management arranged an official opening to mark the completion of the first 45 houses. On this occasion, Lady Campbell of Succoth was on hand to dedicate a foundation stone and Raymond Unwin was one of the principal speakers. Unwin outlined

13. Ibid.

BELOW: Original site plan for Westerton Garden Suburb, only ever partially built.

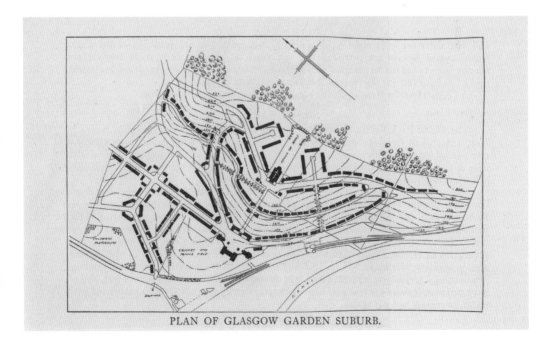

PLAN OF GLASGOW GARDEN SUBURB.

ABOVE: Group of terraced houses in Maxwell Avenue, Westerton Garden Suburb. (Photo: John Reiach)

RIGHT: Detail of English style arts and crafts features in Maxwell Avenue frontage, Westerton Garden Suburb. (Photo: John Reiach)

FACING PAGE

ABOVE: Middle class semi-detached properties in Stirling Avenue, Westerton Garden Suburb. (Photo: J. Rosser)

BELOW: Commemoration stone for the foundation of Westerton Garden Suburb, originally laid by Lady Cambell of Succoth on 19th April 1913. (Photo: J. Rosser)

the recent achievements of tenant co-partnership societies in England and wished the Committee every success in attracting residents. A second phase of construction was undertaken until the end of 1915, when operations were suspended for the duration of WW1. A total of 84 houses had been completed and it was assumed that an additional number of properties would be built once peace was restored. In the event, however, public utility societies found it difficult to achieve the desired results in the economic conditions that prevailed after the war, and Glasgow Garden Suburb Tenants Ltd never managed to realise the original plans for a larger development.

Most of the total stock of 84 houses were built in small terraces of 3 to 8 units.[14] In order to create a mixed-income community, the original rent levels varied from £18 *per annum* for a 2-bedroom non-parlour house to £40 *per annum* for a 3-bedroom parlour house.[15] All of the properties were provided with a bath, and the entire stock was designed with a distinctive arts and crafts character.

Glasgow Garden Suburb Tenants Ltd remained in existence as a co-partnership society for more than 70 years. As with many of the early garden city inspired developments, the need for major repairs became increasingly apparent after WW2. During the 1960s and 1970s, the Committee of Management found it difficult to raise the necessary finance for upgrading and modernisation of the Westerton stock. As

14. East Dunbartonshire Council, Westerton Garden Suburb Conservation Area Appraisal, Draft, January 2011, p. 9.
15. Whitelaw, *A Garden Suburb for Glasgow*, pp. 5-9.

the problem dragged on, a decision was eventually taken in 1988 to proceed with voluntary liquidation in a manner that would allow for the disposal of individual houses through sales to sitting tenants.[16] By this time, Westerton Garden Suburb had been officially designated by the local authority as a Conservation Area and virtually all of the original properties were classified as Category 'B' or 'C' Listed Buildings.[17] In the local authority's most recent Conservation Area Appraisal, the architectural character of the garden suburb is recognised as noteworthy for its 'anglified cottage arts and crafts house designs'.[18]

STIRLING HOMESTEADS

16. East Dunbartonshire Council, Westerton Garden Suburb Conservation Area Appraisal, p. 8.
17. Ibid., p. 3.
18. Ibid., p. 9.
19. Peter Aitken, Cameron Cunningham and Bob Mc-Cutcheon, *Notes for a New History of Stirling: The Homesteads, Stirling's Garden Suburb* (Stirling, 1984), p. 3.
20. Ibid., pp. 8-9.

A small co-partnership development in a rural setting on the edge of Stirling was promoted by another leading member of the Glasgow & West of Scotland Branch, Robert Maclaurin. This development known as Stirling Homesteads aimed to combine garden city style housing with the provision of small holdings on land situated less than two miles from Stirling town centre.[19]

The basic ideas for Stirling Homesteads were conceived at a time when the Board of Agriculture was trying to promote small holdings on Crown Lands.[20] During 1907, the Stirling Branch of the Independent Labour Party (ILP) became interested in linking the provision of small holdings with the construction of attractive cottages. Robert Maclaurin was invited to give a lecture in Stirling on 'Co-operation in House

RIGHT: Co-partnership cottages built by Stirling Homesteads Ltd.

Building' which helped to generate additional interest. He subsequently played a key role in the creation of Stirling Homesteads, using his personal experience in the garden city and arts and crafts movements.[21]

By 1909, a suitable site for the project had been identified in consultation with the Office of Woods and Forests. Stirling Homesteads Ltd was then established as a public utility society operating on co-partnership principles.[22] James Chalmers, a Glasgow-based architect, was appointed to prepare an outline plan for the development.[23] Chalmers had recently entered the design competition mentioned earlier that was sponsored by the Glasgow & West of Scotland Branch of the Garden City Association. His submission was awarded prizes for 'economy in planning' and 'all round design'.

As originally conceived, the project was to include 10 cottages of varying sizes, small holdings and allotments for growing produce, and a working dairy farm of 35 acres.[24] The cottages were to be designed to form a small hamlet within the site. Both the small holdings and the allotments were to be worked on an individual basis. The dairy farm was to be run on a day-to-day basis by a farm manager in paid employment, under the general supervision of a management committee.

By the close of 1910, the 10 cottages were completed and occupied. They were built of brick with harling, and equipped with various fitments designed by members of the Scottish Guild of Handicrafts such as door handles, fireplaces, and letter boxes.[25] The initial group of residents included Robert Maclaurin and John Adams, both of whom were active in the Scottish Guild of Handicrafts, and James Wilson who served as Secretary of the Stirling Branch of the ILP.[26]

The market gardening activities on the allotments and small holdings were generally successful from the outset, but the larger dairy farm struggled to earn a reasonable return. The financial position of the dairy farm grew even worse during the early 1920s, and the Management Committee decided to cease operations in 1926. The co-partnership society continued to perform its housing functions for another 5 decades, until the Crown Commissioners decided to wind up the organisation in 1975.[27]

21. Ibid., p. 15.
22. Ibid., p. 25.
23. Ibid., p. 25.
24. Elizabeth Cumming, *Hand, Heart and Soul: The arts and crafts movement in Scotland* (Edinburgh, 2006), p. 175.
25. Aitken, Cunningham and McCutcheon, *Notes for a New History of Stirling: The Homesteads*, p. 47.
26. Ibid., p. 27.
27. Ibid., p. 48.

COTTAGE DEVELOPMENTS IN THE GREENOCK AREA

The national commitment to naval rearmament had a significant impact on the housing situation within the Greenock area. Additional pressures were placed on the local supply of accommodation as a result of the Admiralty's decision in 1907 to build a new Clyde Torpedo Factory on a site that straddled the boundary between Greenock and Gourock. This facility required a civilian workforce of 700 employees, who were to be provided mainly through the transfer of skilled personnel from the Royal Arsenal at Woolwich in South London. In many cases, these workers were accustomed to living in single-family cottages of a decent standard. Before moving to Scotland, the affected personnel at the Woolwich Arsenal were consulted about their housing preferences. From these discussions, it was apparent that many of the workers were extremely reluctant to live in traditional Scottish tenements.[28]

At the Greenock end, the Admiralty was not prepared to consider taking direct responsibility for housing the incoming civilian workers. It was felt that the growing pressures within the local housing market could not be solely attributed to the opening of the Clyde Torpedo Factory. The generally prosperous trading conditions in the shipbuilding industry were also creating additional demand for working class housing in the Greenock area.[29]

28. Cd. 6192, Seventeenth Annual Report of the Local Government Board for Scotland, 1912–13.
29. Scottish Records Office File DD6/429.

RIGHT: View of Royal Naval Torpedo Factory, Gourock.

FACING PAGE: Terraced cottages in Caledonian Crescent,Gourock, built by Gourock Garden Suburb Tenants Ltd. (Photo: J. Rosser)

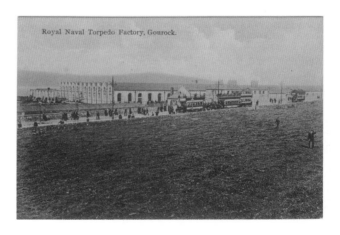

Royal Naval Torpedo Factory, Gourock.

Before the new torpedo factory was fully operational, the Admiralty approached various commercial interests to provide suitable accommodation for workers who were due to be transferred from the Woolwich Arsenal.[30] At this stage, neither the private businesses that were consulted nor the local authorities in the area were prepared to meet this need. The Admiralty then began to explore whether public utility societies might develop the preferred type of cottages. Prior to the declaration of war, 3 cottage developments were undertaken by newly formed co-partnership societies operating in the general vicinity of Greenock and Gourock. The somewhat confusing names of these societies were Gourock Garden Suburb Tenants Ltd, Greenock Garden Suburb Tenants Ltd and Gourock and Greenock Tenants Ltd.

The largest of the 3 developments was undertaken by Gourock Garden Suburb Tenants Ltd at Cove Farm about a half mile to the west of the Clyde Torpedo Factory. In legal terms, this co-partnership society was a subsidiary of the Scottish Garden Suburb Company, which had negotiated an agreement that the Admiralty would cover any losses on the development if it proved difficult to attract a sufficient number of tenants.[31] The parent company was interested in a

30. Ibid.
31. Ibid.

flexible arrangement that would allow the incoming workers a choice of tenure. Essentially, the co-partnership society was intended to cater for those who preferred to be tenants, while the parent company was able to accommodate those who were interested in owning one of the cottages on an individual basis.

Shortly after the Cove Farm site had been acquired from Major Duncan Darroch in July 1911, loan finance was obtained from the Public Works Loan Commissioners. Over the next two years, about 60 cottages were built in Caledonia Crescent and Manor Crescent. In order to clarify how things were progressing within the local housing market, the Local Government Board for Scotland directed its Architectural Inspector, John Wilson, to assess the current situation in 1913. In his assessment, Wilson noted that 48 cottages had already been completed on the Cove Farm site, of which 40 were tenanted and 4 had been purchased by civilian employees at the torpedo factory.[32]

Greenock Garden Suburb Tenants Ltd was active on the east side of Greenock. This co-partnership society had obtained an option on a 30-acre site near Cartdyke station, which was made available at a favourable price by Sir Hugh Shaw Stewart.[33] To enable a cottage development to be built on the site, the landowner was prepared to accept an annual feu duty of only £16 per acre, instead of the usual figure of £70 per acre that was currently being received in cases involving the development of new working class tenements in this part of Greenock.[34] Once loan finance was secured from the Public Works Loan Commissioners, the construction process began in 1913. A terrace of 6 2-storey cottages was initially completed in Bridgend Road, but the co-partnership society never took up the option for additional land. Although the reasons for this decision are not entirely clear, it seems likely that the location was considered to be too distant from the torpedo factory.

Gourock and Greenock Tenants Ltd was formed by the group of workers who had attended the Port Glasgow lecture given by Ebenezer Howard towards the end of 1908. Howard's suggestion that the group should endeavour to provide their desired cottages through their own efforts was taken to heart. About 3 years later, they managed to establish a tenant co-partnership society that was registered for housing purposes under the Industrial and Provident Societies Act. In September 1913, a suitable site within Gourock was acquired from Major Duncan Darroch.[35] The location on the south side of Reservoir Road had commanding views over the Firth of Clyde to Helensburgh. Before the outbreak of WW1, the co-partnership society was able to complete a terrace of 12 2-storey cottages. Although discussions were held with the Admiralty about a second phase of development, this never transpired. Gourock and Greenock Tenants Ltd continued to operate as a co-partnership society until 1965, when a decision was taken to provide opportunities for sitting tenants to purchase their individual properties.

32. Ibid.
33. Cd. 6720, Eighteenth Annual Report of the Local Government Board for Scotland, 1913.
34. Ibid.
35. Scottish Records Office File DD6/1001.

VOLUNTARY DEVELOPMENTS IN OTHER SCOTTISH LOCATIONS

The remaining 4 voluntary sector developments built before the outbreak of WW1 were located in Renfrew, Paisley, West Dunbartonshire and West Lothian. In 3 of these cases, the developments were sponsored by public utility societies set up by concerned employers to ensure that decent housing was available for their workforce in close proximity to places of work.

To the east of Greenock, working class accommodation was also becoming scarce in the Burgh of Renfrew. As the situation worsened, the local authority indicated a willingness to support a tenant co-partnership development by providing a 5-acre site to the east of Paisley Road. Renfrew Garden Suburb Tenants Ltd was established to undertake a development of around 70 units on the site.[36] The properties built in Newmains Road and Beechwood Drive, comprising 1- and 2-storey cottages in short terraces of 4 to 8 units, were initially occupied during the first 6 months of 1914.

To the south of Paisley town centre, the firm of Brown & Polson promoted a public utility society development for employees based at their local works. These 4-in-a-block cottage flats were designed in a distinctive arts and crafts style by T. Graham Abercrombie in 1911 and completed in 1913. A total of 48 units of this type were built on the site in Falside Road, which were described in a Garden City Association report

36. Cd. 7327, Nineteenth Annual Report of the Local Government Board for Scotland, 1914.

RIGHT: Short terrace of cottages in Beechwood Drive, Renfrew, built by Renfrew Garden Suburb Tenants Limited. (Photo: J. Rosser)

ABOVE: Arts and crafts style, 4-in-a-block cottage flats in Falside Road, Paisley, built by Brown & Polson Public Utility Society for local workforce. (Photo: J. Rosser)

LEFT: 4-in-a-block cottage flats in Argyll Park, Alexandria, built by Vale of Leven Tenants Limited. (Photo: J. Rosser)

as containing 'two rooms, with kitchen, scullery, etc., so that the sexes may be decently provided for'.[37] The public utility society established by Brown & Polson was expected to earn less than 3 per cent on the capital invested, a figure well below the return that was normally anticipated for housing developments undertaken on a commercial basis.[38]

37. Ewart G. Culpin, *Garden City Movement Up-To-Date* (London, 1913), p. 28.
38. Ibid.

RIGHT: Miners' cottages in Garden City Bents, near Stoneyburn, built by West Lothian Housing Society.

BELOW: Cottage housing in Garden City Bents today. (Photo: J. Rosser)

In West Dunbartonshire, Vale of Leven Tenants Ltd was formed on a co-partnership basis in May 1913, in order to provide accommodation for workers based at the new Argyle Motor Works in Alexandria. The firm had recently relocated from the centre of Glasgow, and many of the workers were commuting to the new factory by train. According to a local press report, the aim of the co-partnership society was to offer 'something more than a tenement dwelling'. A sizeable site on the edge of Argyll Park was provided by the company for the purpose of developing as many as 250 units. Unfortunately, Argyll Motor Works failed financially during 1914 and the factory premises at Alexandria were sold to the munitions manufacturer Armstrong, Whitworth & Co the following year. In the circumstances only a small group of 4-in-a-block cottage flats was ever completed by Vale of Leven Tenants Ltd This development of 16 units, designed by the well-known Glasgow-based architect James Salmon (Junior), was officially opened in May 1914.[39]

In West Lothian, United Collieries Ltd also took steps to set up a public utility society to provide housing for its local workforce before the onset of WW1. West Lothian Housing Society managed to complete an initial development of miners' cottages to the west of Stoneyburn just prior to the outbreak of hostilities.[40] This development called Garden City Bents involved the construction of 75 single-storey cottages with individual gardens, which have remained popular and well cared for to the present day. During the early 1920s, West Lothian Housing Society managed to complete a second cottage development in the village of Harthill. This initiative formed part of the public utility society response after WW1 which is discussed in Chapter 6.

39. *Glasgow Herald,* 18 May 1914.

40. John B. Murray, *Stoneyburn: The Forgotten Baby* (Wellpark, 1995), p. 11.

5 Scottish Housing and the War Effort

PREVIOUS PAGE: Stone-built terraced cottages in the Fife hamlet of Crombie, provided for civilian employees based at the nearby Royal Navy Armaments Depot. (Photo: John Reiach)

BELOW: Women munitions workers unloading the nitrating pans at the Gretna cordite factory in Dumfriesshire. (Courtesy of the Devil's Porridge Museum Eastriggs)

Although still relatively uncommon in the Scottish landscape, the provision of garden city style housing for working class families became somewhat more familiar through the wartime efforts to accommodate incoming workers. Once war was declared various measures were taken at central government level to expand the supply of housing for civilian defence workers. In key Scottish locations, more than 4,000 permanent and temporary dwellings were produced for this purpose, mainly through the use of emergency powers contained in the Housing Act of 1914.[1]

The accommodation was needed for civilian workers employed in both public and private defence industries. Nearly all of the permanent dwellings were provided in the form of low density cottages or cottage flats, often designed along lines favoured by the garden city movement.[2] Various methods were used to produce the necessary accommodation. In Scotland, a number of different agencies became involved in this effort, including the Local Government Board for Scotland, the Ministry of Munitions, Office of Works, a number of local authorities, a state-sponsored public utility society in the case of Rosyth, and various private sector companies working in partnership with the Local Government Board for Scotland.[3]

The various housing initiatives for civilian defence workers were planned and built at a time of mounting tensions on the home front, particularly within the industrial heartland of Scotland. The underlying reasons for these conflicts were varied and complex but, as Joseph Melling has noted in his writings on the Clydeside rent strikes, the

1. David Whitham, 'State housing and the Great War' in Richard Rodger (ed.), *Scottish Housing in the Twentieth Century* (Leicester, 1989), Appendix 4A, pp. 120-1.
2. Ibid., pp. 102-3.
3. Ibid., pp. 120-1.

growing pressures on the availability and price of housing played an important part. According to Melling,

> Tens of thousands of servicemen were recruited to the forces and left behind dependents on limited incomes. The demand for munitions and armaments brought thousands of migrants to the great industrial and shipbuilding centres of Britain, including the premier shipyard river, the Clyde. Any available housing quickly disappeared as the engineering, shipbuilding and armaments workers were offered almost unlimited overtime. Prices rose more quickly than basic wages and immigrants were forced to pay shortage rents for scarce accommodation near the largest yards and plants.[4]

Against this background, new garden city style developments for civilian defence workers were built in various Scottish locations. The discussion of specific developments begins with brief descriptions of Rosyth and Gretna/Eastriggs, which are generally well covered in the literature. It then focuses on lesser known developments in other parts of Scotland.

4. Joseph Melling, 'Clyde-side rent struggles and the making of Labour politics in Scotland, 1900–39' in Richard Rodger (ed.), *Scottish Housing in the Twentieth Century* (Leicester, 1989), pp. 65-6.

5. Susan Gleave, Influence of the garden city movement in Fife, 1914–23, Unpublished M. Phil., University of St Andrews, 1987, pp. 75-6.

DEVELOPMENT OF ROSYTH

The development process for the Rosyth Royal Naval Dockyard on the Firth of Forth was plagued by lengthy delays. Although the Admiralty had acquired the site on the south-facing coast of Fife early as 1903, construction of the new dockyard did not actually begin until 1909. Once the work had started, progress was hampered by the Admiralty's reluctance to assume any direct responsibility for housing either the construction workforce or the civilian personnel who were to be employed at the dockyard. In the terminology of the Garden City Association, what emerged at Rosyth was essentially a garden village with a dominant single employer rather than a full-scale garden city.

Further complications arose as a result of a policy decision taken by Dunfermline Burgh at the end of 1911. The local authority became committed to the preparation of a town planning scheme for the land

ABOVE: OS map of Rosyth in Fife, published in 1927. (Reproduced with the permission of the National Library of Scotland)

to the south of Dunfermline which included the site for the Royal Dockyard. Nearly two years later, the Admiralty appointed Raymond Unwin to advise on an appropriate pattern of development in the general vicinity of the dockyard.[5] Unwin continued to play an advisory role in the wartime provision of housing at Rosyth. When war was de-

TOP: General view of Rosyth from the south.

RIGHT: Men leaving work through the gates of Rosyth Dockyard.

BOTTOM: Semi-detached cottages in Queensferry Road, Rosyth.

TOP: Terraced housing in Admiralty Road, Rosyth. (Photo: John Rosser)

LEFT: Current state of semi-detached houses in Backmarsh Crescent, Rosyth. (Photo: John Rosser)

BOTTOM: 'Neo-Georgian' terraced housing in Rosyth.

6. Ibid., Chapter 5.
7. Whitham, 'State housing and the Great War', p. 97.
8. Gleave, *Influence of the Garden City Movement in Fife, 1914–23*, p. 105.

ABOVE: Arts & crafts influences in Backmarsh Road, Rosyth (Photo: J. Rosser)

clared in August 1914, the town planning scheme was still awaiting final approval from central government. Nothing in the way of permanent housing for the civilian workforce had been built at Rosyth. In response, the emergency powers defined in the second Housing Act of 1914 were used to establish a public utility society to provide the necessary accommodation.

The public utility society known as the Scottish National Housing Company (SNHC) was set up by the Local Government Board for Scotland in September 1914, with J. R. Findlay, the proprietor of *The Scotsman*, serving as chairman of the management committee.[6] A year later, the first phase of permanent housing construction was under way, comprising 150 units of cottage accommodation designed in the garden city style by the Edinburgh architectural firm of Alfred Greig and Walter Fairbairn.[7] These picturesque 2-storey cottages were built on a triangular site formed by Queensferry Road, Admiralty Road and Backmarch Road. The properties were generally grouped in adjoining terraces of 4 or 6 units, with some semi-detached houses interspersed. An official opening was held in May 1916, at which J. R. Findlay stated that the Rosyth cottages had been designed 'in accordance with English ideas' in view of the great influx of workers from England.[8]

The second phase of construction involving 450 units was designed by Alfred Hugh Mottram (1886–1953) who was employed as in-house architect by the public utility society. Mottram had previously worked as an assistant to Raymond Unwin, on the design of the artisan quarters of Letchworth and Hampstead Garden Suburb.[9] By the time the second phase of construction had been approved, the SNHC was faced with strong pressures to economise. In the circumstances Mottram generally opted for design solutions in the neo-Georgian style and also included a number of 4-in-a-block cottage flats.[10]

In October 1916, the Admiralty acknowledged that 1,000 additional houses were still needed at Rosyth to support the war effort. The construction process was continued and by the time of the signing of the Armistice the SNHC was in a position to report that a total of 1,600 houses had reached the practical completion stage.[11] This figure implies that Rosyth was clearly the largest of Scotland's wartime permanent housing developments. The results, however, were at best a mixed success. Various complaints were registered by the original group of tenants concerning excessive rent levels, inconvenient rear access for properties built in adjoining terraces, cramped internal spaces and problems of uncomfortable draughts within the dwelling.[12]

From the standpoint of garden city design, it is appropriate to mention another wartime housing development about 5 miles west of Rosyth. This housing was linked to the establishment of a Royal Navy Armaments Depot near the hamlet of Crombie during 1912. Three years later, the Office of Works built a small stone-built development of 2-storey cottages for civilian employees based at the Depot. These properties are situated along the A95 and in Ordnance Road and Central Road leading off the A95. Approximately 35 cottages were provided in short terraces of 4 and 8 units, with whinstone rubble facades which seem well suited to this part of the Scottish landscape.

PERMANENT HOUSING AT GRETNA AND EASTRIGGS

In 1915, the Ministry of Munitions set up a new cordite factory in Dumfriesshire, on a remote site near the villages of Gretna and Eastriggs. Housing and community facilities for the workforce were to be provided by the Ministry's own Department of Explosives Supply, under the supervision of Raymond Unwin.[13] Resident architect for the project was Courtney M. Crickmer (1879–1971), who had previously worked with

9. Ibid., pp. 106-9. Mottram remained in Scotland. After the closure of the Royal Dockyard in 1925, he provided architectural services for the Second Scottish National Housing Company, which was set up by central government as a separate body to assist local authorities with non-traditional forms of residential construction. Mottram was later appointed as Consulting Architect for the Scottish Special Areas Housing Association when it was established in 1937.
10. Ibid.
11. Ibid., pp. 123-4.
12. Whitham, 'State housing and the Great War', p. 98.
13. Swenarton, *Homes fit for Heroes*, p. 58.

RIGHT: OS map of Gretna
Township, published in 1951.
(Reproduced with the permission
of the National Library of
Scotland)

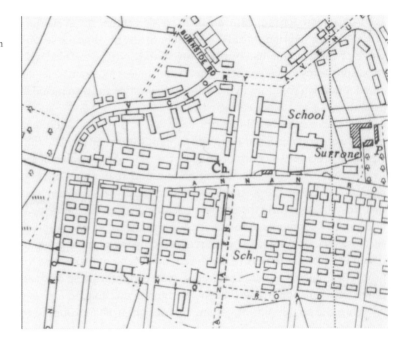

14. Ibid., p. 58.
15. Ibid., p. 60.

Unwin at Letchworth and Hampstead Garden Suburb.[14] The initial brief
envisaged the development of several types of living accommodation for
13,500 civilian workers, along with shops, laundry, central kitchen, post
office, cinema, meeting hall, dental clinic, institute, school and churches.[15]

At the outset, the plan was to meet the housing needs of the work-

RIGHT: View of Central Avenue,
Gretna Township as seen today.
(Photo: J. Rosser)

TOP: Hostel accommodation built in Central Avenue, Gretna Township, which was subsequently converted to individual houses.

LEFT: The Green, Eastriggs.

BOTTOM: Street view of Ladysmith Road, Eastriggs.

force by constructing a limited range of temporary accommodation. Three types of prefabricated timber huts were to be provided: 4-room family units for married workers, small hostels for 9 workers and a housekeeper, and larger barracks for as many as 70 to 80 workers.[16] In May 1916, the Minister of Munitions Dr. Christopher Addison made a site visit to observe how the project was progressing, and shortly after his visit decided that some permanent housing should be built.[17] This decision was partly influenced by the rising cost of timber, which had narrowed the margin of difference between the cost of temporary and permanent construction. A high standard of permanent accommodation was to be provided at Gretna and Eastriggs, however, the results were also expected to demonstrate the potential economic advantages of simplification and standardisation.

In the circumstances, Unwin and Crickmer responded by experimenting with a style of working class housing that was sometimes labelled 'the People's Georgian'. By the end of WW1, a total of 310 permanent houses had been built at Gretna and Eastriggs Townships.[18] At Gretna, the permanent accommodation was located to the north of the town centre and along the main road leading west to Eastriggs. Gretna was clearly the larger of the two townships, but Eastriggs had a greater proportion of permanent housing.

According to Mark Swenarton, this was the first large-scale demonstration of the potential advantages of simplified design.[19] The permanent housing in both communities consisted mainly of semi-detached cottages and short terraces of 4 to 6 units, finished in brick or roughcast. Many of the properties had a boxlike character, with simple hipped roofs that had no dormers or other breaks in the eaves line. Although the design solutions were consciously understated, a sense of variety was achieved through imaginative grouping of houses and inventive details for porches and lintels. Interestingly, a number of 2-storey brick hostels were constructed in a form that would allow for easy conversion to individual terraced cottages after the war.[20]

For military reasons, the developments at Gretna and Eastriggs were undertaken in an atmosphere of relative secrecy. The wartime housing initiatives of the Local Government Board for Scotland were implemented more openly, since many of the sites were located near to existing factories and shipyards.

16. John Minett, 'Government sponsorship of new towns: Gretna 1915-17 and its implications' in Richard Rodger (ed.), *Scottish Housing in the Twentieth Century* (Leicester, 1989), p. 108.
17. Swenarton, *Homes Fit for Heroes*, pp. 58-9.
18. Ibid., p. 59.
19. Ibid., p. 60.
20. Minett, 'Government sponsorship of new towns: Gretna 1915–17 and its implications', p. 109.

WARTIME DEVELOPMENTS IN LANARKSHIRE

Lanarkshire's heavy industries made a vital contribution to the war effort. As the number of incoming workers increased, a collaborative housing response was agreed by the Local Government Board for Scotland, the Ministry of Munitions, Lanark County Council, and the Mid-Lanark District Committee.[21] William Whyte, who was the driving force behind the development of local authority cottage accommodation for miners before the war, also played a key role in meeting the needs of civilian defence workers. The collaborative response for civilian defence workers involved the construction of over 500 low density units on 6 different sites. This work was carried out in two distinct phases.

The first phase began in October 1915. Under the general supervision of the Local Government Board for Scotland, the Mid-Lanark District Committee agreed to build 200 houses on 3 sites in the vicinity of Mossend. In return for a measure of financial assistance to offset the cost of construction, the Ministry of Munitions received an option to nominate tenants for the duration of the war.

21. Cmd. 230, Twenty-fourth Annual Report of the Local Government Board for Scotland, p. xxxii.

BELOW: Site of war memorial within Local Government Board for Scotland development at the junction of Park Street and Coronation Road East, in the general vicinity of Mossend. (Photo: J. Rosser)

22. Ibid.

One of the 3 developments, involving 100 units, was located off North Road in what are now known as Rowanden Avenue, Stanley Drive, and Mavisbank Avenue (originally named Verdun Street, Suvla Drive and Jutland Street, respectively). The second development, involving 50 units, was located off Calder Road, in Avon Drive, Cadzow Drive, Clyde Drive and Douglas Drive. To the southeast, in the New Stevenson area, the third development of 50 units was completed along Coronation Road and in Park Street.[22] These areas generally contained a mix of 4 structure types built in brick: single-storey semi-detached cottages, 2-storey semi-detached cottages, short terraces of 2-storey cottages, and 4-in-a-block cottage flats.

A second phase of construction was agreed at the close of 1916,

BELOW: Layout plan for Local Government Board for Scotland model housing scheme off Duke Road, Cambuslang.

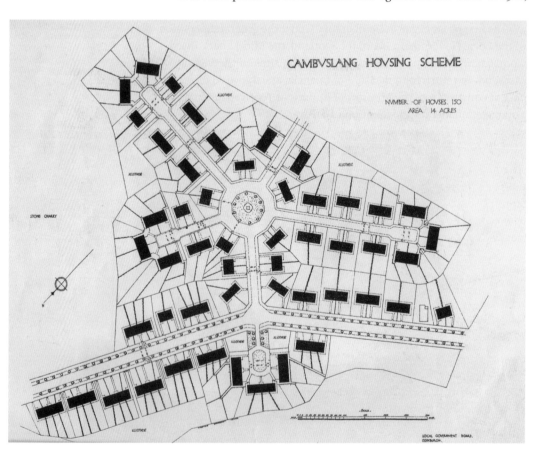

CAMBVSLANG HOVSING SCHEME

NVMBER ·OF· HOVSES. 150
AREA 14 ACRES

with a somewhat different pattern of working relationships. For these
additional developments, the Local Government Board for Scotland
assumed direct responsibility for construction of the housing, on the
understanding that the stock would be transferred to local authority
ownership within 7 years of the conclusion of the war, at a price based
on current market value.[23] Until the change in ownership occurred,
the Ministry of Munitions and the local authority were to be jointly
responsible for managing and maintaining the properties.

During the second phase of construction approximately 300 units
were built on 5 different sites. The range of available house types was
similar to the mix created for the first phase developments. The largest
project undertaken during the second phase involved the construction
of 150 units within the Cambuslang area, off Duke's Road. This development was one of 3 'model schemes' promoted by the Local Government

23. Ibid., p. xxxiii.

Board for Scotland on sizeable parcels of land that could be used to demonstrate site planning principles along garden city lines. Looking to the future, these model schemes were intended as benchmarks for working class housing provision after the war. The main part of the Cambuslang development to the east of Duke's Road, was designed as a cluster of cul-de-sacs named Cathkin Place, Fraser Street, Cathkin Avenue, Whyte Avenue (named for William Whyte), and Quarry Place.[24]

A smaller development of 50 units was built within the wider Cambuslang area, to the north of the model scheme, in Fullarton Avenue and Lloyd Avenue.[25] The remaining 3 developments were built in the vicinity of Mossend. The earlier projects at Calder Road and Coronation Road were extended by 50 and 24 units, respectively, and another new development comprising 76 units was built to the south of Holytown Road in Thankerton Avenue, Central Avenue, and Woodhall Avenue.[26]

24. Ibid.
25. Ibid.
26. Ibid.

BELOW: Local authority cottage provision for incoming civilian defence workers in Brown Street, Greenock. (Photo: J. Rosser)

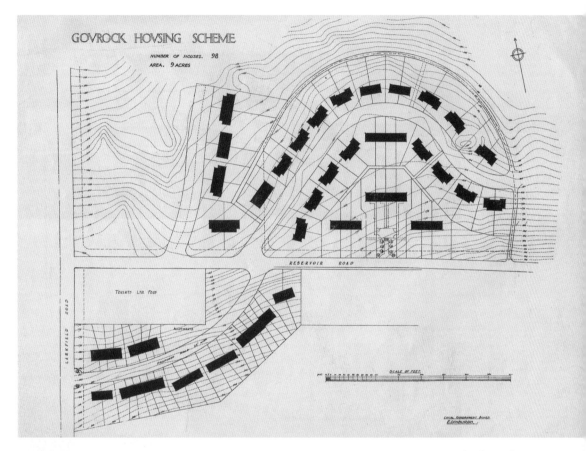

GOVROCK HOVSING SCHEME

NUMBER OF HOUSES. 98
AREA. 9 ACRES

RESERVOIR ROAD

TENANTS LTD. FEUS

ALLOTMENTS

LARKFIELD ROAD

SCALE OF FEET.

LOCAL GOVERNMENT BOARD.
EDINBURGH.

WARTIME DEVELOPMENTS AT GREENOCK AND GOUROCK

ABOVE: Layout plan for Local Government Board for Scotland model housing scheme in Reservoir Road, Gourock.

Housing market pressures persisted in the Greenock area, in spite of the pre-1914 initiatives of public utility societies. The Local Government Board for Scotland continued to monitor the situation during the early stages of the war and eventually decided that additional housing was needed for incoming workers. At the start of 1916, Greenock Town Council was persuaded to build a cottage development at Craigieknowes to accommodate civilian employees of the Admiralty.[27] The Local Government Board for Scotland approved the plans for this development and provided general supervision during the construction stage. Financial support in the form of a discretionary

27. Ibid., p. xxxii.

28. Ibid., p. xxxii.
29. Ibid., p. xxxii.

TOP: Short terrace of cottages in Reservoir Road, Gourock, built as part of Local Government Board for Scotland model housing scheme.

BOTTOM: Further provision for incoming civilian defence workers in Admiral Nelson Road, Gourock, built in conjunction with Local Government Board for Scotland model housing scheme. (Photos: J. Rosser)

capital grant was received from the Admiralty.

The Craigieknowes cottages were located to the east of Greenock town centre, nearby the recent co-partnership development of Greenock Garden Suburb Tenants Ltd. The site for the 102 cottages was developed at a density of 13 units per acre, with a mix of 2-storey semi-detached houses and short terraces of 4 adjoining 2-storey units.[28] All of the local authority cottages in Grosvenor Road, Baxter Street and Brown Street contained a living room and 3 bedrooms, along with a scullery, bathroom, larder, and coal cellar.[29]

Although the Craigieknowes cottages represented a significant increase in the supply of housing available to civilian employees of the Admiralty, additional accommodation was still needed to meet the needs of the Clyde Torpedo Factory workforce. In response to this situation, the Local Government Board for Scotland took a decision in August 1916 to build another low density development in Gourock on behalf of the Admiralty. This project, involving a total of 98 units, was also one of the 3 model schemes promoted by the Local Government Board for Scotland. It was constructed in two phases on a 9-acre sloping site in Reservoir Road, adjacent to the recent co-partnership development of Greenock and Gourock Tenants Ltd. In order to take full advantage of the views across the Firth of Clyde, a number of the properties were designed with the back elevation to the street and the living room overlooking the estuary.[30]

Given the sloping character of the land, the streets leading off Reservoir Road were designed to follow the natural contours of the site. In order to demonstrate the potential advantages of open planning, the average density for the development was limited to 11 units per acre.[31] Along Reservoir Road, and in Rodney Road and Nelson Road leading off to the north and Grenville Road leading off to the south, the main forms of housing were 2-storey semi-detached cottages and small terraces of 3, 4, and 6 single-family units. In the second phase of construction, a limited number of 4-in-a-block cottage flats were included in the interest of economy. A varied mix of house sizes was provided, including 2-bedroom units with a living room, 3-bedroom units with a living room, and 3-bedroom units with a living room and parlour.

30. *Local Government Board for Scotland, Provision of Houses for the Working Classes after the War* (Edinburgh, 1918), p. 10.
31. Ibid.

OTHER LOCAL GOVERNMENT BOARD FOR SCOTLAND PROJECTS

During the course of WW1, the Local Government Board for Scotland was responsible for another 5 developments of permanent housing in various parts of Scotland. These projects were undertaken at Glengarnock in Ayrshire, Inchinnan in Renfrewshire, Alexandria in West Dunbartonshire, Invergordon on the Cromarty Firth, and Clydebank immediately to the west of Glasgow.

The Glengarnock development, located immediately to the

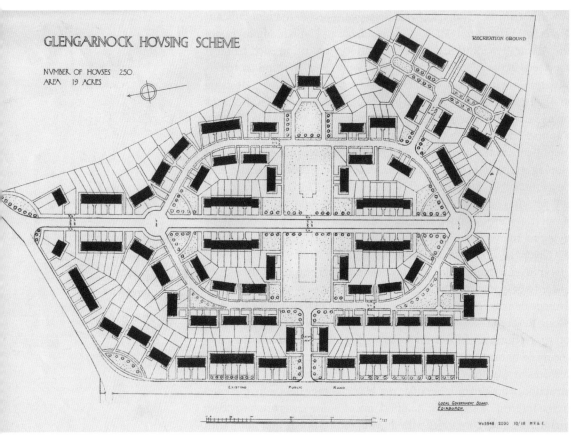

GLENGARNOCK HOVSING SCHEME

NVMBER OF HOVSES 250.
AREA 19 ACRES

RECREATION GROUND

EXISTING   PVBLIC   ROAD

LOCAL GOVERNMENT BOARD,
EDINBVRGH.

W·5948 2000 10/18 M?E&E.

ABOVE: Layout plan for Local
Government Board for Scotland
model housing scheme at
Glengarnock /Kilbirnie, North
Ayrshire.

RIGHT: View of cottage
accommodation in Dalry Road,
Glengarnock, built as part of
Local Government Board for
Scotland model housing scheme
for incoming defence workers.

DALRY ROAD, KILBIRNIE

ABOVE: Cottage provision in Dalry Road, Glengarnock today. (Photo: J. Rosser)

south of the village of Kilbirnie, was also one of the 3 model schemes promoted by the Local Government Board for Scotland. It was implemented in collaboration with the Ministry of Munitions, in order to provide 250 houses for workers based at the Colville and Company steel works.[32] In 1916, the Colville firm gifted a 19-acre site for the purpose and agreed that, if Ayrshire County Council was not interested in taking ownership of the properties after the war, the Company would purchase the accommodation at current market value. Given the relatively remote location of the site, various problems were encountered in obtaining the necessary labour and materials for completion of the project.

The Glengarnock site was developed at a density of 13 units per acre, with attention given to grouping of houses, pleasant street vistas, and reservation of land for community facilities. The stock of housing was built along the east side of Dalry Road and immediately to the east within an oval configuration of streets called Western Crescent, Central Avenue and Eastern Crescent, with a cul-de-sac leading off named South Neuk. Approximately three-quarters of the properties were built of brick to provide a mix of 2-storey semi-detached cottages, short terraces of adjoining single-family cottages and 4-in-a block cottage flats. The remainder were single-storey semi-detached cottages constructed of

32. Cmd. 230, pp. xxxiii-xxxiv.

33. Ibid., pp. xxxiv-xxxv.
34. Ibid., pp. xxx-xxxi.

concrete slabs. As a rule, the properties built on the Glengarnock site contained 2 or 3 bedrooms.

In Renfrewshire, to the east of Erskine, the Admiralty asked the Local Government Board for Scotland to provide suitable housing for civilian workers based at Inchinnan airship factory operated by Beardmore & Company.[33] This request was made during 1915. It eventually resulted in a collaborative development of 50 brick-built houses known as Beardmore Cottages. Architectural plans were prepared by the technical staff of the Local Government Board for Scotland. Thereafter, the Company assumed responsibility for the construction process under the general supervision of the Local Government Board. A mix of single-storey cottages, 2-storey cottages, and 4-in-a-block cottage flats were provided on the site. The range of house sizes included properties with 1 to 3 bedrooms plus living room, scullery, bathroom and larder.

To the north of the Clyde estuary, in Alexandria, the Local Government Board for Scotland developed 150 houses on behalf of the Admiralty for civilian employees of the munitions manufacturer Armstrong, Whitworth & Company, which had acquired the former Argyll Motor Works.[34] This project was implemented during 1916 on a site in the Levenvale area, near to the small group of cottage flats that was recently built by Vale of Leven Tenants Ltd. Initially, the plan was to build temporary wooden huts, but it was soon realised that a much better standard of housing could be provided at only marginally greater cost using a durable form of light construction. Many of these properties were allocated to Belgian refugees who had become involved in the

LEFT: View of warships in Invergordon harbour during World War 1.

CENTRE LEFT: Local Government Board for Scotland development known as Admiralty Cottages, Invergordon.

CENTRE RIGHT: Houses in Murray Road today, built as part of Admiralty Cottages development, Invergordon. (Photo: J. Rosser)

LEFT: Local Government Board for Scotland cottage provision in George Crescent, Clydebank. (Photo: J. Rosser)

production of explosives. This accommodation remained in use until the mid-1930s, when the local authority carried out a phased process of redevelopment that enabled the existing residents to be rehoused on site in newly built council properties.

The Local Government Board for Scotland responded to another request from the Admiralty in 1916 which resulted in the provision of 126 units of cottage accommodation for civilian defence workers employed at the Invergordon Naval Base on the Cromarty Firth.[35] This development, known as Admiralty Cottages, was built on a site to the east of Invergordon, north of Saltburn Road. All of the properties were single-storey semi-detached cottages constructed of concrete block, located in Golf View Terrace, Cadboll Road, Elliot Road, Grosvenor Street, Inglis Road and Murray Road.

35. Ibid., p. xxxi.
36. Ibid., p. xxxiv.

At the start of 1918, the Local Government Board for Scotland responded to a request from the Ministry of Munitions to provide housing for civilian defence workers based at the Singer factory in Clydebank.[36] This development of 100 houses was planned by the technical staff of the Local Government Board for Scotland in consultation with the Burgh of Clydebank. The local authority agreed to purchase the properties at current market value within 3 years of the end of hostilities. The Office of Works took responsibility for the construction process, and the necessary accommodation was built on a site to the east of Kilbowie Road, in Clarence Street, George Crescent, George Avenue, Lloyd Street (later renamed Robert Burns Avenue) and Riddell Street. All of the stock consisted of 2-storey brick-built cottages that were usually arranged in pleasant groups of 4 adjoining units.

Virtually a century has now passed since the wartime housing described in this chapter was originally produced. As part of the background research for this book, site visits to all of the various developments were undertaken to clarify the existing state of the housing. With the exception of the accommodation at Alexandria, which was replaced in the 1930s, all of the wartime developments were still fully occupied and well cared for by the current residents.

In the majority of cases, the first tenants of this wartime housing built in the garden city style would have been incoming workers previously based in England. Over the years, however, a substantial number of Scottish households will have benefited directly from this popular form of accommodation, which began to demonstrate an attractive alternative to tenement living for working class families. During the 1920s, a majority of the developments sponsored by the Local Government Board for Scotland were transferred to local authorities. During the 1980s, the properties in public ownership would have become eligible for purchase by sitting tenants under the Right-to-Buy legislation. As a consequence, many of the wartime housing developments are now overwhelmingly in the private sector and transferring at values that are well beyond the reach of those on limited incomes.

6

1919 Act Homes Fit for Heroes in Scotland

PREVIOUS PAGE: Local authority 1919 Act development in Wylie Avenue, Alexandria, West Dunbartonshire, designed by Joseph Weekes who went on to become one of Scotland's outstanding public sector architects of the inter-war period. (Photo: John Reiach)

BELOW: Distinctive development known as Esher Cottages, built in 1920 by The Scottish Veterans' Garden City Association in the former county of Perthshire at Stirling Road, Callander.

After WW1 various measures were taken at central government level to deliver on the electoral promises of 'Homes Fit for Heroes'. The statutory framework for British housing policy was revised significantly to enable an effective response in the prevailing conditions. The required amendments were conceived at Westminster and applied with only minor variations in England, Wales and Scotland.[1] At a difficult time of transition to peacetime production, local authorities were expected to play a much more proactive role in addressing the housing needs of working class households. Given the unusually high level of construction costs, innovative forms of financial assistance were to be provided by central government in order to facilitate a desirable standard of low density development along garden city lines.

The specific arrangements for confronting Scottish conditions were defined in the Housing and Town Planning Etc. (Scotland) Act of 1919. In Scotland, as in England and Wales, priority was to be given to the elimination of housing shortages by expanding the general supply of accommodation for working class families. In the Scottish case, the application of garden city design principles within urban areas usually implied a major shift from tenement to cottage construction.

This chapter is primarily concerned with documenting the house-building experience of Scottish local authorities and public utility societies under the short-lived provisions of the Housing and Town Planning (Scotland) Act of 1919. As noted earlier, the relatively generous subsidy arrangements of the 1919 Act were officially withdrawn in 1921 as part of a wider package of austerity measures. Although the

1. Marian Bowley, *Housing and the State 1919–1944* (London, 1945), Appendix 1, p. 267.

physical achievements of the 1919 Act developments were regarded as disappointing in quantitative terms, the general standard of provision was seen to be impressive in qualitative terms. Many of these developments have remained popular symbols of the 'Homes Fit for Heroes' campaign as well as noteworthy examples of garden city influences on the built form of working class housing in Scotland.

TUDOR WALTERS REPORT AND SCOTTISH CONDITIONS

When the Tudor Walters Committee was first appointed in July 1917, the scope of investigation was limited to the construction of working class dwellings in England and Wales. Several weeks later, the final report of the Ballantyne Royal Commission on Housing in Scotland was formally submitted to the government for consideration. When the brief of the Tudor Walters Committee was subsequently amended to include Scotland in April 1918, J. Walker Smith, the Chief Engineering Inspector of the Local Government Board for Scotland, was added to the panel. At the end of October, the final report of the Tudor Walters Committee was submitted to the President of the Local Government Board.

In addressing issues relating to Scotland, the Tudor Walters Committee tended to reinforce the main findings of the Ballantyne Royal Commission. Differences in habits, living arrangements and standards of provision were clearly acknowledged in the Tudor Walters Report, as follows:

In reference to Scotland . . . the existing conditions and traditional habits of the people differ from those in England and Wales, the people having been accustomed to a more limited number of rooms, often individually of larger size in the more northern country. The house with two bedrooms is such an improvement on the accommodation which is available for a very large number of the inhabitants of Scotland at the present time, that it would represent in Scotland an advance in conditions more marked than would be represented by the 3-bedroom cottage in England.[2]

2. Cd. 9191, Report of the Committee to Consider Questions of Building Construction in connection with the Provision of Dwellings of the Working Classes in England, Wales and Scotland, p. 26. (Tudor Walters Report)

The continuing influence of the tenement tradition, and the difficulties in shifting to lower density forms of working class provision, were also recognised, as follows:

> . . . a large portion of the population have formed the habit of living in flats and are so attached to having their whole dwelling on one floor, that it would be too sudden a break with habits and conditions to attempt to build nothing but the 2-storey cottage.[3]

Members of the Tudor Walters Committee were aware that the Ballantyne Commission had argued against a total ban on tenement construction and had put forward various suggestions for the reform of tenement design. In the circumstances, the Tudor Walters Committee chose not to offer any further advice on the reform of tenement design. Although it was expected that cottage flats would be more popular in Scotland than in England and Wales, there was only one illustration in the Tudor Walters Report relating to 'double-flatted houses'.[4]

As John Frew has observed, the design guidance within the Tudor Walters Report focused mainly on the arrangement of interior space within the dwelling.[5] Relatively few architectural elevations were actually shown in the final publication. In terms of external design, the key to desirable results was seen to be the involvement of competent professional architects, who would be able to respond sensitively to site conditions and to select appropriate local building materials. Design competitions were considered to be an effective way of identifying qualified architects who were committed to the challenge of designing attractive forms of low density housing for working class families.

3. Ibid., p. 25.
4. Ibid., p. 24.
5. John Frew, 'Towards a municipal housing blueprint: the architects' panel competition and its aftermath 1918–1919', *Architectural Heritage* XI, 2000, pp. 43-54.

ARCHITECTURAL COMPETITIONS

Once the Tudor Walters Committee had been appointed, the Local Government Board and the Royal Institute of British Architects organised a design competition in November 1917 to stimulate interest in the design of working class housing in England and Wales. This competition was exclusively concerned with design solutions for single-family cottages. The results were announced a year later, and the winning entries were subsequently presented in a publication titled *Cottage Design*.[6]

In August 1918, a separate design competition was organised by the Local Government Board for Scotland and the Institute of Scottish Architects.[7] This competition was intended to focus on a range of structure types that were seen to be relevant in the Scottish context. In the circumstances, it was regarded as important to give some attention to the reform of tenement design as well as the provision of cottage flats.

All of the entrants to the Scottish competition were provided with two recent publications as background information. One publication was a memorandum which had been issued by the Local Government Board for Scotland, describing the key features of the model schemes built for civilian defence workers at Gourock, Cambuslang, and Glengarnock.[8] The other publication was a report prepared by the Women's House-Planning Committee, which was appointed to assess a number of the wartime housing developments in Scotland from 'the housewife's standpoint'.[9] The Women's House Planning Committee was chaired by Helen L. Kerr, who had also served as a member of the Ballantyne Commission. The panel also included two of Glasgow's leading housing activists, Mary Barbour and Mary Laird. The Women's Committee argued that more houses with a parlour should have been provided in the developments that were evaluated. The Committee's report also noted that, during the course of site visits, many tenants had expressed a strong preference for semi-detached cottages.

The Scottish architectural competition was structured with reference to 4 types of housing: single-storey cottages, 2-storey cottages, 2-storey cottage flats, and 3-storey tenements. The winning entries were presented to the public at the Royal Scottish Academy in Edinburgh, as part of the Spring Exhibition of 1919.[10] This display was titled 'The Housing Question'. A number of the commended designs were included in a joint publication of the Local Government Board for Scotland and the Institute of Scottish Architects, which appeared in June 1919 under the title *Housing of the Working Classes in Scotland*.[11] Among the recipients of premium awards were John A. W. Grant, who had designed the housing at Westerton Garden Suburb before WW1, Messrs. Greig and Fairburn who produced the first phase of wartime housing at Rosyth, and Messrs. Stewart and Paterson who went on to design an impressive small development at Callander for The Scottish

6. Royal Institute of British Architects, *Cottage Designs* (London, 1918).

7. Frew, 'Towards a municipal housing blueprint'.

8. Local Government Board for Scotland, *Provision of Houses for the Working Classes After the War*.

9. Local Government Board for Scotland, Report of the Women's House Planning Committee (Edinburgh, 1918).

10. Frew, 'Towards a municipal housing blueprint'.

11. Local Government Board for Scotland, *Housing of the Working Classes in Scotland* (Edinburgh, 1919).

Veterans' Garden City Association.

The competition was intended to identify a group of competent architects that were available and interested in designing local authority housing in Scotland. In practice, however, relatively few of the successful entrants received an opportunity to design the 1919 Act developments eventually produced. As John Frew has noted, by the time the winning entries were announced, many of the larger Scottish authorities had already appointed architects for their initial developments, and many of the smaller Scottish authorities chose to use local architectural practices for this type of work.[12]

ADMINISTRATIVE AND FINANCIAL ARRANGEMENTS

12. Frew, 'Towards a municipal housing blueprint'.

The development process for 1919 Act housing was closely administered by central government. This approach was applied throughout Great Britain for several reasons. Many local authorities were seen to lack experience in direct housebuilding. Tight supervision was also seen to be warranted on financial grounds.

In the immediate aftermath of WW1 the costs of residential construction were abnormally high, and it was recognised that affordable housing for working class families could not be produced without a substantial level of subsidisation. As a consequence, Treasury assistance was to be provided for the creation of general needs housing for the first time in England, Wales and Scotland, with central government carrying the major share of the financial burden. As noted earlier, under the provisions of the Housing and Town Planning Etc. (Scotland) Act of 1919, the annual financial contributions of Scottish local authorities were restricted to an amount equivalent to a levy of four-fifths-of-a-penny on the local rates. Any remaining operating losses on the newly created 1919 Act stock were the responsibility of central government.

When the 1919 Act was first approved by Parliament, the housing and town planning functions north of the Border were administered by the Local Government Board for Scotland. In 1920, however, the Local Government Boards throughout Britain were wound up as part of a more general reorganisation of central government. In Scotland, the administrative responsibilities for housing and town planning were transferred to a new agency known as the Scottish Board of Health. The official targets for the required level of housebuilding in Scotland were essentially based on the Ballantyne Commission findings, which suggested that approximately 120,000 new houses were needed to remove the general shortage of accommodation and an additional 120,000 units were needed to deal with the most extreme cases of overcrowding and to replace properties regarded as unfit for human habitation.[13]

The Ballantyne Commission regarded these targets as a conservative estimate of Scotland's needs, appropriate for a first significant response to the historic legacy of poor housing. In the prevailing economic conditions, however, these targets were to prove ambitious, and it was hoped that public utility societies would be able to make a substantial contribution to the overall housebuilding effort. With this in mind, a new system of capital grants for developments sponsored by public utility societies was also introduced in the main 1919 Act and subsequently raised in the in the Housing (Additional Powers) Act of 1919. The level of grant aid for public utility society developments was the same in England, Wales and Scotland.

Although the Coalition Government was nominally committed to removing the existing shortages of housing, no effective measures were taken to ensure that the required supplies of labour and materials were available to facilitate the desired levels of housing construction. Not surprisingly, in the absence of effective controls on the construction sector of the economy, the rate of housing completions was generally disappointing. In the circumstances, while the short-lived financial provisions of the 1919 Act were available, Scottish local authorities managed to build a total of only 25,000 houses and Scottish-based public utility societies were only able to produce another 500 houses. Although this level of output was well short of the official targets, in many cases the 1919 Act developments were genuinely impressive in qualitative terms.

Within Scotland, over 300 separate developments were completed using the provisions of the 1919 Act. These developments of working class housing represented a sharp break with the Scottish tenement tradition. Although sometimes regarded an imposition of English style housing by central government, the low density developments built along garden city lines have remained highly popular over the longer term. Although often seen as the physical expression of the 'Homes Fit

13. Cd. 8731, p. 9.

for Heroes' spirit, however it appears that relatively few of the returning veterans were able to gain access to this impressive new standard of working class accommodation.[14]

In the face of abnormally high cost of construction, the generous subsidies on offer were still not sufficient to allow the rents to be set at affordable levels for unskilled workers and poorer households. In the absence of additional assistance in the form of rent rebates, the 1919 Act local authority properties were usually allocated to skilled industrial workers, artisans and lower-salaried white collar employees who could be expected to meet their rent obligations. Although the Scottish Board of Health advised that discharged soldiers and sailors should receive priority in allocating the newly built stock, in many local authorities the house-letting decisions were vetted by local councillors who were particularly concerned to ensure that the occupants would be able to meet their rent obligations.

PROFILE OF LOCAL AUTHORITY COMPLETIONS

As noted above, Scottish local authorities managed to produce a total of 25,000 houses under the financial provisions of the Housing and Town Planning (Scotland) Act of 1919. Virtually all of these houses were completed and occupied by 1925. From information contained in the annual reports of the Scottish Board of Health, it is possible to summarise the general characteristics of the 1919 Act local authority stock built in Scotland.[15] The following discussion focuses on the broad geographic pattern of development, the number of bedrooms provided, the range of house types and the method of construction.

Relative to the pre-1914 pattern of local authority housebuilding in Scotland, the geographic distribution of 1919 Act housing was far more widespread. This change in the broad spatial pattern of local authority accommodation did not occur by chance. It reflected both the new statutory duty that was placed on local authorities, and the pressures applied by the Scottish Board of Health to achieve the agreed house-building targets. Of the total number of local authority completions, the proportion of houses built outwith burghs, in small settlements and rural areas, was as high as 30 per cent.[16] The remaining 70 per cent were

14. For comments on this issue, see J. Frew, *Housing the Heroes* (Kirkcaldy, 1987), p. 8; and Barrhead Community Council, *Housing the Heroes* (Barrhead, c. 1985), p. 44.

15. Unfortunately, similar information for all English and Welsh authorities was not published in the corresponding annual reports of the Ministry of Health.

16. Cmd. 2156, Fifth Annual Report of the Scottish Board of Health, 1924, p. 126.

175

spread widely across the Scottish burghs, with Glasgow and Edinburgh accounting for only 25 per cent of the 25,000 units.

The 1919 Act local authority stock was provided for general needs, in an effort to expand the available supply of working class accommodation. The principal concern was to produce a desirable standard of new housing for households with children, and for this reason central government guidance stressed that houses containing less than 2 bedrooms would only be approved in exceptional circumstances. Local authorities were urged to provide a substantial proportion of units with 3 or more bedrooms, in order to allow male and female children to sleep in separate rooms. At the outset, local authorities in Scotland were given a notional target for the desired mix of house sizes. Each local authority was expected to ensure that 50 per cent of their total completions contained 2 bedrooms, 40 per cent 3 bedroom, and 10 per cent contained 4 or more bedrooms.[17]

In many cases, local authorities found it difficult to comply with this policy. Given the historic pattern of over-crowding in Scotland, and the general reluctance to increase household expenditure on rent, many of the initial applicants for the new 1919 Act units were primarily interested in properties containing 2 bedrooms. In the face of mounting pressures to produce results, the Scottish Board of Health relaxed the original house size targets. According to the outturn figures for total completions by Scottish local authorities, 2 per cent of the 1919 Act units contained 1 bedroom, 57 per cent contained 2 bedrooms, 35 per cent contained 3 bedrooms, and the remaining 6 per cent contained 4 bedrooms or more.[18] In contrast, for all English and Welsh authorities, a sizeable majority of the 1919 Act local authority units contained at least 3 bedrooms.

With regard to structure types and density levels, the Scottish Board of Health appears to have followed the recommendations of the Ballantyne Commission. In putting forward proposals for 1919 Act developments, Scottish local authorities were able to gain approval for the construction of single-family cottages, cottage flats, and pavilion-style tenements of up to 3 storeys. Across the whole of Scotland, nearly two-thirds (63 per cent) of the local authority 1919 Act completions were single family cottages, built either in short terraces or as semi-detached pairs.[19] Four-in-a-block cottage flats were relatively common throughout Scotland, in a range of house sizes. Cottage flats accounted for

17. Cmd. 825, First Annual Report of the Scottish Board of Health, 1920, p. 14.
18. Cmd. 2156, p. 126.
19. Cmd. 2416, Sixth Annual Report of the Scottish Board of Health, 1924–25, p. 36.

31 per cent of the total number of completions, while the remaining 6 per cent were non-traditional forms of tenement.

Central government guidance on building methods generally favoured brick construction. However, in many parts of Scotland, good quality bricks and experienced bricklayers were in very short supply. As the rate of local authority completions lagged behind the official housebuilding targets, the Scottish Board of Health began to consider other building methods, so long as the estimated costs of construction were not excessive. Approved tenders covering the first 18,000 local authority units indicate that brick construction was used for more than 80 per cent of this stock.[20] Stone construction, or a combination of brick and stone, was used to build 11 per cent of the units, and other methods of concrete or timber construction were used for the remaining 6 per cent. Some of Scotland's most attractive developments of 1919 Act housing were produced in locations where the local authority was able to make a viable economic case for stone construction.

20. Cmd. 1319, Second Annual Report of the Scottish Board of Health, 1921, p. 139.

LOCATIONS OF SPECIFIC LOCAL AUTHORITY DEVELOPMENTS

One of the key aims of the background research for this book was to identify the specific locations of developments built by Scottish local authorities under the Housing and Town Planning (Scotland) Act of 1919. This investigation was not straightforward since the original records for these developments were not retained at central government level and there does not appear to be a comprehensive list of approved developments for the whole of Scotland.

Fortunately, it was possible to locate the vast proportion of 1919 Act local authority developments by searching old valuation rolls which are now accessible in digital form at the National Archives of Scotland in Edinburgh. Once the relevant locations and street addresses were identified, it was possible to consult various digital mapping sites on the internet to obtain a better understanding of the characteristics of the housing and local street patterns.

This systematic search of valuation-roll data revealed as many as 300 separate local authority developments in different parts of the country

SPATIAL DISTRIBUTION OF 1919 ACT LOCAL AUTHORITY HOUSING DEVELOPMENTS

SCOTLAND

Shetland

Number of
Developments

• 1
● 2–4
⬤ 11

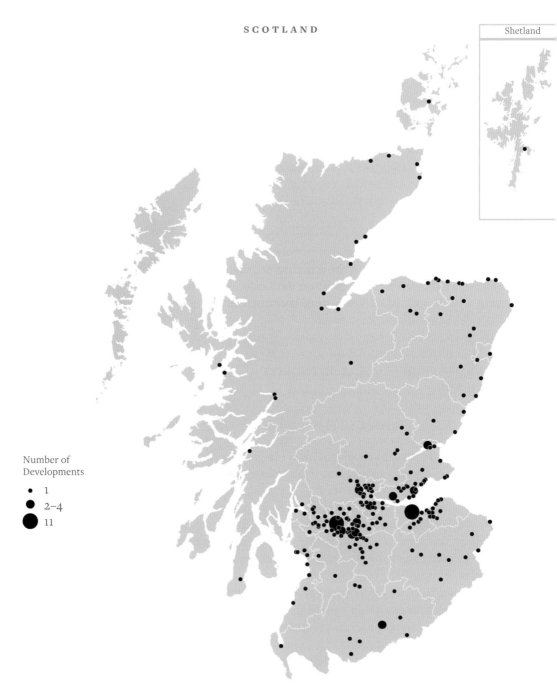

(see map on facing page for specific locations). The developments in question varied widely in scale, from a handful of houses in relatively remote locations to as many as 1,500 houses for the largest single case in a major city. For a substantial share of the 300 locations, site visits were undertaken to obtain additional information and to observe the current state of the properties.

Within the scope of this book, it is not possible to describe all of the individual 1919 Act local authority developments that were identified. In order to give a flavour of the basic character of Scotland's 'Homes Fit for Heroes', the following section profiles a selected group of developments in urban and rural settings.

A SELECTION OF LOCAL AUTHORITY DEVELOPMENTS

This discussion focuses initially on key examples in larger settlements, and then looks at some of the experience in smaller towns, villages, and rural areas. Like the housing built for civilian defence workers during WW1, the 1919 Act local authority developments have generally remained highly popular and are now predominantly owner-occupied as a result of Right-to-Buy sales to sitting tenants.

Within the major cities, Glasgow managed to produce by far the largest amount of 1919 Act housing for general needs. Nearly 5,000 units were built within Glasgow, including sizeable developments to the north of the River Clyde in Riddrie/Kennyhill and Gilshochill and to the south of the river in Govanhill, Craigton, Drumoyne, Elder Park, and Mosspark. Edinburgh produced a total of 1,200 units, including sizeable developments such as Chesser and Hutchison on the west side of the city, Boswall on the north side of the city and Northfield on the east side of the city. Dundee built 3 developments, of which the largest was Logie, to the west of the city centre, which is claimed locally as the first 1919 Act development completed in Scotland. In Aberdeen, the largest development of 1919 Act accommodation was in the Torry area south of the harbour.

Noteworthy developments were also built within other large settlements such as Clydebank (in the Kilbowie area), Dumfries (in the Cresswell area), Dunfermline (Brucefield), Kilmarnock (Piersland

FACING PAGE: Map showing the geographic spread of 1919 Act local authority housing developments across Scotland.

Park), Motherwell (North Lodge), Perth (Muirton), Renfrew (Victory Gardens), St Andrews (Bassaguard) and Stirling (Riverside).

With regard to built form, semi-detached cottages and short terraces of single-family units comprised the bulk of the housing stock within the developments at Mosspark, Kilbowie, Brucefield, Piersland Park, North Lodge, Bassaguard, and Riverside. At the scale of 1,500 units, Glasgow's Mosspark was by far the largest 1919 Act development built in Scotland and the clearest Scottish example of a self-contained garden suburb.

In the case of Chesser in Edinburgh and Logie in Dundee, virtually all of the accommodation consisted of 4-in-a-block cottage flats. Unusually, at Muirton in Perth, most of the units were provided within 2-storey tenements. Both Northfield in Edinburgh and Riddrie/Kennyhill in Glasgow had a mix of structure types that included 3-storey tenements, but there were some striking differences in layout and design. At Northfield, along each street frontage, there was usually a variety of structure types, whereas at Riddrie/Kennyhill there were 3 distinct sub-areas, one consisting of 3-storey tenements, another consisting of 4-in-a block cottage flats, and a third consisting of single-family cottages.

For the most part, the housing within these developments in larger settlements was built of brick and harling, often with design details influenced by the arts and crafts movement. At Victory Gardens in Renfrew and Brucefield in Dunfermline, however, many of the properties had exposed brickwork with minimal forms of decoration, giving a neo-Georgian character favoured by the Tudor Walters Committee. A number of the developments included some form of stone construction, however, only Chesser in Edinburgh and Cresswell in Dumfries were predominantly built in stone. The housing in the Bassaguard area of St Andrews was constructed of concrete blocks, using the Winget method to give a rusticated stone-like external appearance.

The garden suburb of Mosspark, on the edge of Glasgow's Bellahouston Park, included a wide range of community facilities. Within the site boundaries, ample amounts of land were reserved for a school, a church and church hall, bowling greens and local shops. At Riddrie/Kennyhill, to the northeast of Glasgow city centre, a sizeable bowling green was provided, while in Dundee at Logie a communal heating system was included within the development along with a large swathe of open space and a monumental viewing platform at one end. In Edinburgh, at Chesser, an area for allotments was provided for the use of residents as an integral part of the development. It is difficult to know how much attention was originally given to landscaping, but the visual effects of mature trees were particularly noted during site visits to Brucefield, Kilkbowie, Mosspark and Piersland Park.

Some of the most charming Scottish examples of 1919 Act local authority housing were built in less populous settlements and rural areas, often by county councils. Distinctive small developments can be found in many parts of Scotland, however, the results in East Lothian, Fife, Aberdeenshire and Sutherland are particularly impressive.

In East Lothian, the architectural practice of J. M. Dick Peddie and Walker Todd was responsible for a series of attractive developments at Dirleton (Fidra Avenue), Gullane (Hopetoun Terrace), Longniddry (Elcho Road/Terrace) and Macmerry (St Germains Terrace). In the Kingdom of Fife, two of the most interesting examples are located at East Wemyss (Glebe Park) and Leven (Scoonie Crescent/Drive). In the coastal villages of Aberdeenshire and Sutherland, the small stone-built developments at Portknockie (Admiralty Street), Golspie (Seaforth Road), and Brora (Manse Park) are particularly well adapted to the local setting.

Other examples of well-crafted stone-built developments can be found in the Borders at Galashiels (Forest Avenue/Gardens), in West Dunbartonshire at Alexandria (Wylie Avenue), in Dumfriesshire at Lockerbie (Victoria Park) and in Shetland at Lerwick (Breiwick Road). The development at Alexandria was designed by Joseph Weekes, the County Architect, who made a number of later contributions in West Dunbartonshire which are discussed in Chapter 7.

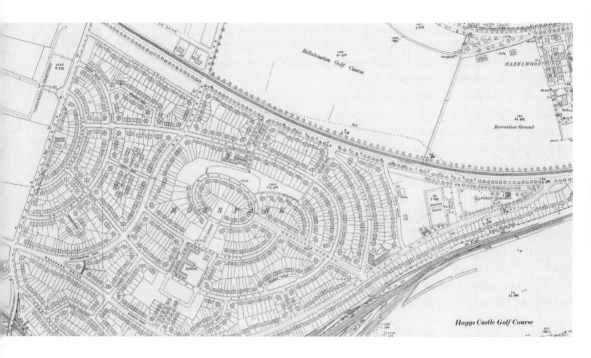

ABOVE: OS map of Mosspark area
of Glasgow published in 1936.
(Reproduced with the permission
of the National Library of
Scotland)

TOP: View of Mosspark housing at the junction of Bellahouston Drive and Mosspark Drive.

CENTRE: Corkerhill Road in the early days.

BOTTOM: Typical low density cottage provision in Mosspark. (Photo: J. Rosser)

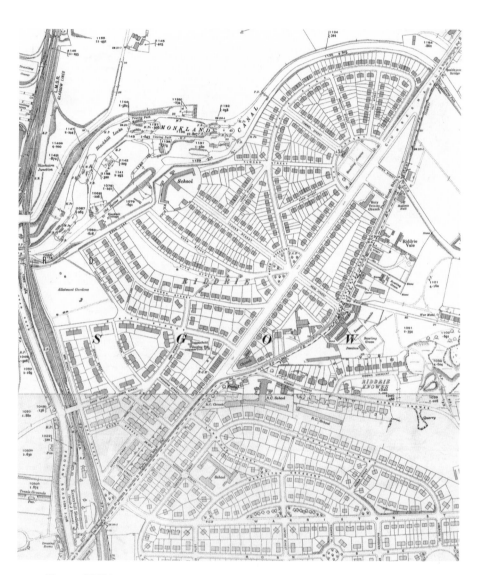

ABOVE: OS map of Riddrie area
of Glasgow published in 1935.
(Reproduced with the permission
of the National Library of
Scotland)

TOP LEFT: View of Gala Street, Riddrie in the 1920s.

BOTTOM LEFT: Three-storey pavilion-style tenements built in Kennyhill during the early 1920s.

TOP RIGHT: 4-in-a-block cottage flats in the middle section of Riddrie/Kennyhill.

BOTTOM RIGHT: Current view of Kennyhill tenements.

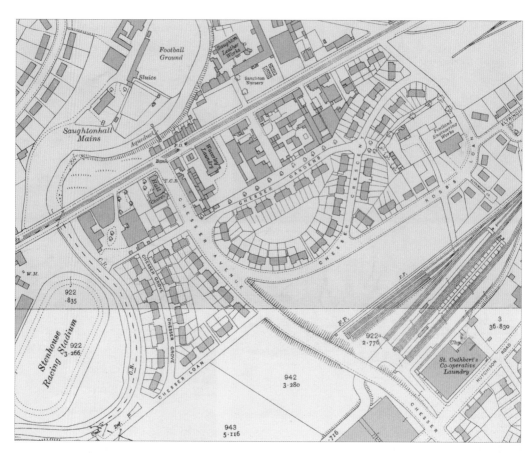

ABOVE: OS map of Chesser area
of Edinburgh published in 1933.
(Reproduced with the permission
of the National Library of
Scotland)

RIGHT: Allotments provided within
the centre of Chesser are still
being used productively.

LEFT: View of 1919 Act housing in Chesser Gardens, Edinburgh, shortly after construction.

BELOW: Stone-built 4-in-a-block properties in Chesser Avenue, with bags of character and upper flats intended for larger families.

ABOVE: OS map of the Northfield
area of Edinburgh published
in 1934. (Reproduced with the
permission of the National Library
of Scotland)

ABOVE: Northfield's 1919 Act stock included a number of free standing 3-storey tenements with 6 flats, which over the years have remained popular places to live.

LEFT: Attractive grouping of cottages with small green in Northfield Crescent.

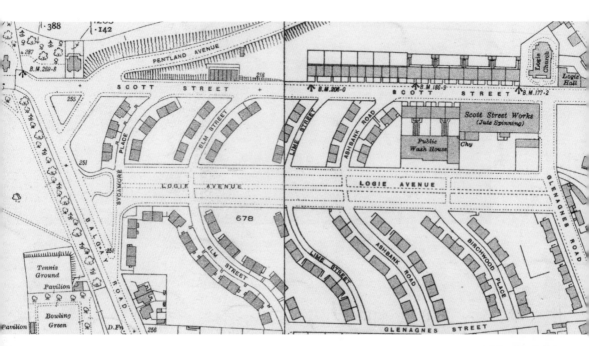

ABOVE: OS map of Logie area
of Dundee published in 1939
and 1941. (Reproduced with the
permission of the National Library
of Scotland)

RIGHT: Plaque commemorating
the official opening of the Logie
development and the earlier
turning of the first sod by Sir
George McCrae, legendary WW1
hero and Vice-President of the
Local Government Board for
Scotland.

ON 27TH MAY 1920 SIR WILLIAM DON. K.B.E.,
LORD PROVOST AND LORD LIEUTENANT OF DUNDEE,
FORMALLY OPENED THE DWELLING HOUSES
ERECTED UNDER THE LOGIE SCHEME
FOR THE HOUSING OF THE WORKING CLASSES,
THE FIRST SOD ON THE SITE HAVING BEEN TURNED BY
SIR GEORGE McCRAE, D.S.O.,
VICE-PRESIDENT OF THE LOCAL GOVERNMENT BOARD FOR SCOTLAND,
ON 4TH JULY 1919,
THIS HOUSING SCHEME BEING THE FIRST IN SCOTLAND
TO BE PROCEEDED WITH BY A LOCAL AUTHORITY
IN PARTNERSHIP WITH THE STATE.

TOP LEFT: General view of Logie, reputed to be the first 1919 Act local authority housing scheme in Scotland.

TOP RIGHT: Looking east from the viewing platform along the major Logie Avenue green strip.

BOTTOM LEFT: Street view of Sycamore Place. (Photo: J. Rosser)

BOTTOM RIGHT: 4-in -block cottage flats with all entrance doors at the side of the building.

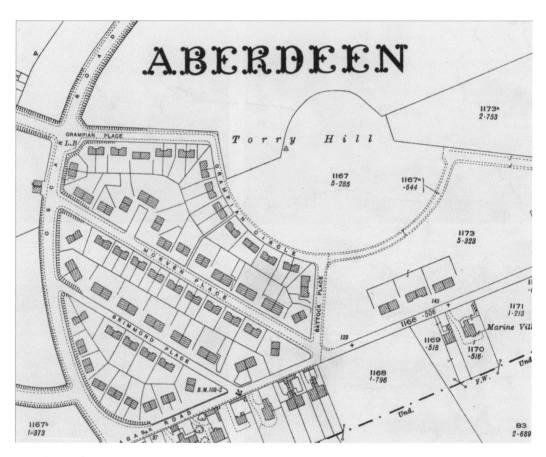

ABOVE: OS map of Torry area
of Aberdeen published in 1926.
(Reproduced with the permission
of the National Library of
Scotland)

RIGHT: Semi-detached houses
in Brimmond Place. (Photo: J.
Rosser)

ABOVE: Street view along part of Grampian Circle.

LEFT: Use of granite construction in Morven Place. (Photo: J. Rosser)

1919 Act Homes Fit for Heroes in Scotland:
A Selection of Local Authority Developments

DUMFRIES | CRESSWELL

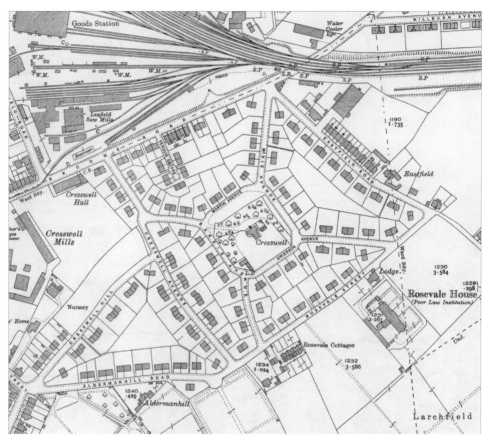

ABOVE: OS map of Cresswell area of Dumfries published in 1931. (Reproduced with the permission of the National Library of Scotland)

RIGHT: Red sandstone frontages along Alderman Hill. (Photo: J. Rosser)

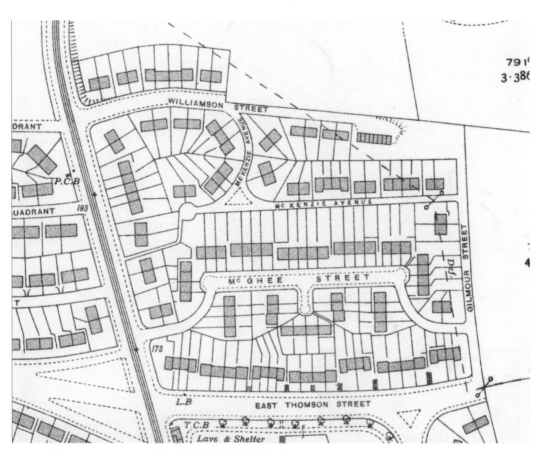

ABOVE: OS map of Kilbowie area of Clydebank published in 1939. (Reproduced with the permission of the National Library of Scotland)

LEFT: McGhee Street properties enhanced by mature trees. (Photo: J. Rosser)

DUNFERMLINE | BRUCEFIELD

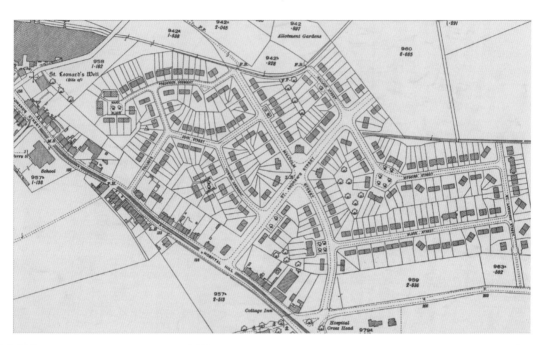

TOP: OS map of Brucefield area of Dunfermline, published in 1926. (Reproduced with the permission of the National Library of Scotland)

LEFT: View along Pitcairn Street. (Photo: J. Rosser)

RIGHT: Semi-detached houses in Malcolm Street with brickwork details uncommon in Scotland. (Photo: J. Rosser)

ABOVE: OS map of Piersland Park area of Kilmarnock published in 1939. (Reproduced with the permission of the National Library of Scotland)

LEFT: Cul-de-sac of semi-detached cottages off Melville Street. (Photo: J. Rosser)

1919 Act Homes Fit for Heroes in Scotland:
A Selection of Local Authority Developments

PERTH | MUIRTON

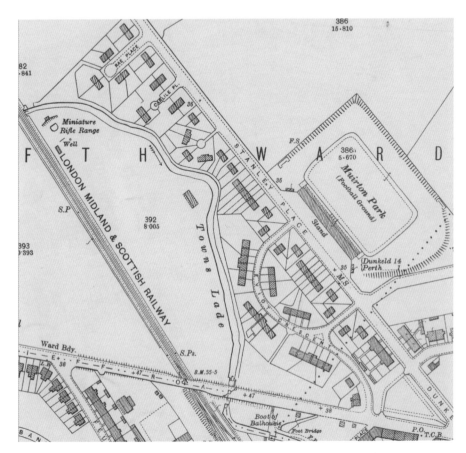

RIGHT: OS map of Muirton area of Perth published in 1932. (Reproduced with the permission of the National Library of Scotland)

BELOW LEFT: Well maintained 2-storey tenements in Eviot Crescent. (Photo: J. Rosser)

BELOW RIGHT: Children's play area accessed from Eviot Crescent. (Photo: J. Rosser)

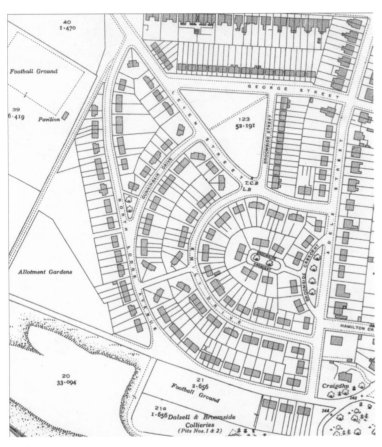

ABOVE: OS map of North Lodge area of Motherwell published in 1939. (Reproduced with the permission of the National Library of Scotland)

LEFT: View at junction of Leven Street and Cunningair Drive. (Photo: J. Rosser)

1919 Act Homes Fit for Heroes in Scotland:
A Selection of Local Authority Developments

RENFREW | VICTORY GARDENS

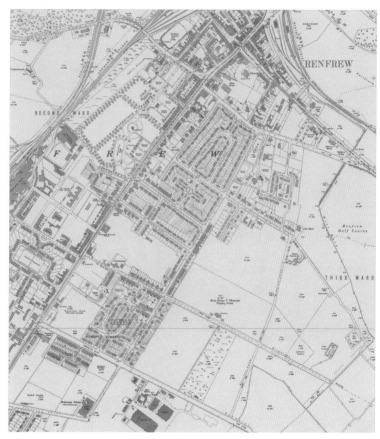

RIGHT: OS map of Victory Gardens area of Renfrew published in 1947. (Reproduced with the permission of the National Library of Scotland)

BELOW: Mix of harled and exposed brickwork in Loanhead Avenue. (Photo: J. Rosser)

ABOVE: OS map of Riverside area of Stirling published in 1947. (Reproduced with the permission of the National Library of Scotland)

LEFT: Short cul-de-sac of semi-detached cottages off Waverley Crescent. (Photo: J. Rosser)

DIRLETON | GULLANE

TOP: Dirleton cottages designed by
J M Dick Peddie and Walker Todd.
(Photo: J. Rosser)

RIGHT: 1920s view of stone-built
houses in Hopetoun Terrace,
Gullane also designed by Dick
Peddie and Walker Todd.

BOTTOM: Hopeton Terrace
properties as they appear today.
(Photo: John Reiach)

ABOVE: Another 1919 Act development designed by Dick Peddie and Walker Todd in Elcho Terrace, Longniddry. (Photo: J. Rosser)

LEFT: Dick Peddie and Walker Todd were also responsible for the development in St Germains Terrace, Macmerry. (Photo: J. Rosser)

BELOW: Small group of 1919 Act cottages in the distance at East Saltoun. (Photo: John Reiach)

1919 Act Homes Fit for Heroes in Scotland:
A Selection of Local Authority Developments – Fife

ST ANDREWS | LEVEN | EAST WEMYSS

RIGHT: St Andrews development in the Bassaguard area, built using the Winget method of concrete block construction. (Photo: J. Rosser)

CENTRE LEFT: Municipal bowling green provided in the centre of Scoonie development at Leven.

CENTRE RIGHT: Current view of Scoonie Drive. (Photo: J. Rosser)

BOTTOM: East Wemyss development in Glebe Park. (Photo: J. Rosser)

GOLSPIE | BRORA | PORTKNOCKIE | LERWICK

LEFT: Golspie development in Seaforth Road (Photo: J. Rosser)

CENTRE LEFT: Brora development in Manse Park. (Photo: J. Rosser)

CENTRE RIGHT: Admiralty Street houses in the distance at Portknockie, Aberdeenshire (Photo: J. Rosser)

BOTTOM: View of Lerwick development in the Breiwick Road area, from across the bay. (Photo: J. Molloy)

LOCKERBIE │ GALASHIELS │ ALEXANDRIA

ABOVE LEFT: Lockerbie development at Victoria Park in the 1920s.

ABOVE RIGHT: Victoria Park today. (Photo: J. Rosser)

RIGHT: Galashiels development in Forest Gardens. (Photo: J. Rosser)

BELOW: Alexandria development in Wylie Avenue and surrounding streets. (Photo: J. Rosser)

PUBLIC UTILITY SOCIETY DEVELOPMENTS

New funding provisions for public utility society developments were also included in the Housing and Town Planning Act of 1919. This legislation made available a central government subsidy for individual housing projects sponsored by registered public utility societies. Financial assistance was offered in the form of a lump sum grant covering up to 30 per cent of approved development costs. This level of subsidisation was considerably less generous than the financial arrangements on offer to local authorities. In an effort to stimulate a greater response by public utility societies throughout Great Britain, an amendment was included in the Housing (Additional Powers) Act of 1919 which raised the capital grant on offer to a figure of 50 per cent of approved development costs.[21]

21. Cmd. 825, p. 25.

Despite this increase, the general response by registered public utility societies in the early 1920s was seen to be disappointing. Within a given locality, any existing or potential public utility societies were in effect competing with the local authority to provide new accommodation at rents that skilled working class households could afford. Given the prevailing high costs of construction, very few of the experienced public utility societies felt that a 50 per cent capital grant was sufficient to enable a desirable standard of housing to be developed at rents comparable to the amounts that the local authorities would be charging for 1919 Act accommodation.

In Scotland, registered public utility societies managed to produce a total of only 500 houses using the available funding provisions. These new developments were undertaken by fewer than 10 different bodies, of which only one had been active in the years before the outbreak of WW1. Three of the societies were sponsored by employers interested in providing suitable accommodation for their workforce – Kinlochleven Village Improvement Society in the West Highlands, Burntisland Public Utility Society in Fife, and West Lothian Housing Society which had previously built Garden City Bents near the West Lothian village of Stoneyburn.

Kinlochleven Village Improvement Society was established with the support of the British Aluminium Company. At the outset, it was hoped that as many as 200 cottages could be built at Kinlochmore using the available grant aid. In the event, however, significant difficulties were experienced in obtaining the remainder of the capital required for the project. Only 24 units were actually completed before the 1919 Act funding provisions were withdrawn, however, the Kinlochmore development was eventually expanded when the financial provisions for registered public utility societies were restored under the Housing Act of 1923.

Burntisland Public Utility Society was established by Burntisland Shipbuilding Company in an effort to provide desirable accommodation for their employees in a convenient location. This development of 20 properties in Kirkcaldy Road and Dallas Avenue was predominantly built in the form of 4-in-a-block cottage flats. West Lothian Housing Society sponsored a second development for miners employed by United Collieries in the village of Harthill, comprising 36 2-storey cottages in Polkemmet Road, Burns Crescent and Stanley Road.

Four additional public utility society developments were undertaken in Dundee, Glasgow and Edinburgh, by groups that were particularly interested in promoting affordable opportunities for owner-occupation. In Dundee, the Dundee Garden City Association managed to complete a sizeable development of 82 cottages to the north of Kingsway, which were made available to potential owner-occupiers. This housing in Clive Road, Bruce Road and Foster Road consisted mainly of semi-detached properties. The garden city influence was especially apparent on several corner sites, where 3 adjoining units were designed in a manner reminiscent of the early work of Barry Parker and Raymond Unwin at Brentham Garden Suburb.

On the south side of Glasgow, in the Newlands area, Glasgow Public Utility Society sponsored a development of 74 stone-built, semi-detached cottages for owner-occupation. These properties containing 3 and 4 bedrooms were built in the vicinity of Merrylee Road and Glasserton Road. In Edinburgh, two smaller projects for owner-occupation were undertaken by registered public utility societies. To the northwest, near Davidson's Mains, Barnton Public Utility Society completed a development of 10 semi-detached cottages in Barnton Gardens. To the east, near Portobello, Joppa Building Society completed an interestingly designed group of 8 cottage flats in Morton Street, off Joppa Road.

TOP: Kinlochmore development by
Kinlochleven Village Improvement Society.
(Photo: J Rosser)

ABOVE LEFT: Burntisland development in
Kirkcaldy Road by Burntisland Public
Utility Society. (Photo: J. Rosser)

ABOVE RIGHT: Harthill development by West
Lothan Housing Society. (Photo: J. Rosser)

TOP LEFT: Early view of Downfield development by Dundee Garden City Association.

TOP RIGHT: Example of garden city influence on Downfield design. (Photo: J. Rosser)

BOTTOM LEFT: Part of Newlands development on the south side of Glasgow by Glasgow Public Utility Society. (Photo: J. Rosser)

BOTTOM RIGHT: Barnton Gardens development in the western suburbs of Edinburgh by Barnton Public Utility Society.

Although the level of response by public utility societies was seen to be disappointing in Scotland, one organisation known as The Scottish Veterans' Garden City Association (SVGCA) has made a long-standing effort to provide suitable accommodation for severely injured service personnel. This organisation was founded in 1915 by a concerned group of individuals within Edinburgh's business community who wished to help veterans returning to the home front after suffering severe injuries on active duty during WW1. At the outset, various forms of assistance were considered before the group decided to focus on the creation of housing and employment opportunities.[22]

The first recorded meeting of the group was held in May 1915. It was convened by an Edinburgh tailor named Alexander Sim, whose son Alistair Sim later became a renowned film actor. Within a matter of months, SVGCA was formally launched and steps were taken to extend the network of volunteers to other parts of Scotland. A number of prominent Scots became involved, including Lord Edward Salvesen, who lost two sons in the war, and Sir Henry Ballantyne, who chaired the Royal Commission on Housing in Scotland that was appointed in 1912.

At an early stage, visits were made to learn more about Letchworth and other recent garden city developments in England. Initially, the organisation aimed to create small settlements in rural settings, with garden city style cottages that were specially designed to meet the needs of severely injured veterans. The vision was that those who had directly experienced the horrors of war would appreciate and benefit from a peaceful existence in the countryside. It was also hoped that life in a rural setting would offer various opportunities for the development of new skills within a mutually supportive community.

Between 1915 and 1930, SVGCA developed a decentralised network of 15 local branches known as district committees. These local affiliates were directly responsible for identifying feasible sites, selecting and briefing architects, and managing any houses that were completed within the given catchment area. In a number of instances, local authorities provided valuable support for the district committees. A total of 20 developments, containing nearly 220 houses, were completed in various parts of Scotland, including the cities of Aberdeen, Dundee, Edinburgh, Glasgow and Perth; the larger towns of Bathgate, Falkirk, Greenock, Haw-

22. This discussion of the early development of The Scottish Veterans' Garden City Association is based upon information contained in minute books, annual reports and other records which are held at the organisation's registered office in Edinburgh.

ick, Montrose and Peebles; and the smaller communities of Blairgowrie, Bonnyrigg, Callander, East Calder, Longniddry, Moffat, Pitlochry and St Boswells. These early SVGCA developments varied in size from 2 to 33 cottages. Two-thirds of the developments contained fewer than 10 units.

During the first 4 years of operation, SVGCA was funded entirely by voluntary contributions, including generous donations from Caledonian Societies and other support groups based in North America. When the Housing and Town Planning Act of 1919 received parliamentary approval, the organisation decided to take advantage of the capital grants on offer to registered public utility societies. In order to qualify for this type of financial assistance, a subsidiary called The Scottish Garden City Housing Society was legally established as a public utility society operating under the general supervision of SVGCA.

The first SVGCA development, located in the East Lothian village of Longniddry, was based on the organisation's rural vision. This initiative was launched in 1918, and implemented in phases over a 12-year period. A total of 33 cottages were built in Kitchener Crescent, Aberlady Road, and Wemyss Terrace, along with a small community hall, a workshop, tea rooms, allotments, poultry runs, piggeries and a fruit farm. Although the cottage accommodation was greatly appreciated by the original occupants, other aspects of the initiative were regarded by the residents as less successful. It soon became apparent that, for many of the veterans, the nature of their injuries would not allow them to carry out the types of work on offer in an efficient or enjoyable manner. In addition, a substantial number of the residents had grown up in urban areas and would have preferred to live near to their families in locations that provided a wider range of opportunities for education and employment. Fortunately, SVGCA volunteers were committed to monitoring the satisfaction levels of the initial group of residents and this feedback generated a change of direction in the development of future projects. In light of the Longniddry experience, the bulk of the subsequent SVGCA developments were located in more suburban settings on the periphery of larger settlements.

Although the district committees were free to choose their own architects, an impressive standard of housing provision was generally achieved. Careful attention was given to the design specifications for the cottages, as well as the layout of public and private open space. The cottages provided by the district committees contained features

ABOVE: WW1 flag day fundraising badge to promote the work of The Scottish Veterans' Garden City Association. The lower image shows the reverse side.

that were innovative for the time, such as generous doorways to allow easy access. Many of the 2-storey properties also had a bedroom and a specially designed bathroom on the ground floor.

In a number of cases, the architectural treatment of the early SVGCA developments was particularly distinctive. The cottages at Longniddry were designed in an arts and crafts manner by the Edinburgh-based practice of James Henry and Thomas Maclennan. Most of these properties now have a listing of Category B. The firm of Henry and Maclennan also prepared the general development plan for Earl Haig Gardens in Edinburgh, which was built on a site in the Trinity area provided by the family of Lord Salvesen. This plan involving a quadrangle of 31 houses around a small common green was completed in 3 phases between 1920 and 1922. The first and third phases were designed in a neo-Georgian style by Henry and Maclennan. The second phase was designed in an arts and crafts manner by the Edinburgh practice of Burnet Orphoot, Frank Whiting and William Bryce. All of the houses at Earl Haig Gardens now have a listing of Category C.

ABOVE: Period photo of Lord Edward Salvesen and Alexander Sim, key figures in the formation of The Scottish Veterans' Garden City Association.

Two of the Perthshire developments were designed by the Glasgow-based practice of John Stewart and George Paterson. At Callander, the development known as Esher Crescent was launched in 1920 with the support of the Town Council and Lord Esher. These 12 stone-built cottages, incorporating Scottish neo-vernacular details that resemble the work of Robert Lorimer, now have a listing of Category B. At Pitlochry, the development known as Rie-Achan was completed in 1922 on a site about a half mile from the centre of the town. These 8 stone-built cottages in a more open setting now have a listing of Category C.

The various district committees continued to promote new initiatives for severely injured veterans of WW1 to the end of the 1920s. After WW2, a vigorous effort was again made to expand the supply of accommodation for service personnel who had suffered severe injuries. SVGCA has remained in operation as a registered Scottish charity, with an extended remit to build and maintain housing for selected individuals (and their dependents) who have served in either the British armed forces, the merchant navy, or the police or fire brigades, and have become partially or totally disabled while on active duty or after completion of service. At the time of writing, SVGCA was providing more than 600 houses in over 70 Scottish locations, from the Border with England north to the line of the Great Glen.

TOP: Terraced houses at Park Road, Bonnyrigg, by Orphoot, Whiting and Bryce (Photo: J. Rosser)

CENTRE LEFT: Multiple views of Longniddry development in the 1920s.

CENTRE RIGHT: Detail of cottages in Kitchener Crescent, Longniddry. (Photo: J. Rosser)

RIGHT: Centrepiece of Callander development in Esher Crescent. (Photo: J. Rosser)

TOP: Neo-Georgian terrace within Edinburgh development at Earl Haig Gardens. (Photo: J. Rosser)

LEFT: Architectural drawing of neo-Georgian terrace by Henry and Maclennan.

BELOW: Panorama of Pitlochry development known as Rie-Achan. (Photo: J. Rosser)

7 Wider Garden City Influences in Inter-War Scotland

PREVIOUS PAGE: Detail of Braehouse in the Dunbartonshire Village of Rhu, one of the outstanding 1930s local authority developments designed by County Architect Joseph Weekes. (Photo: John Reiach)

BELOW: Panorama of late 1930s local authority cottage development in Seafield Crescent on the western edge of Dunbar, by John A. W. Grant who retained a lifelong interest in garden city design. (Photo: J. Rosser)

The material in this final chapter covers a number of related themes, including the changing pattern of residential development during the inter-war period, the continuing impact of garden city ideas on the built form of Scottish working class housing, the evolving activities of campaigning organisations with an interest in housing and town planning, and the emerging demands for better coordination of policies relating to housing, town planning and economic development.

Generally speaking, the 1919 Act local authority housing discussed in the previous chapter had a dramatic effect on the physical character of the built environment, especially on the periphery of Scotland's larger cities and towns. Although the number of completions was well below the official central government targets, the standard of provision was unprecedented for working class accommodation and the open pattern of development created a sharp visual break with the tenement tradition. The best of the 1919 Act developments have come to be recognised as tangible achievements of the 'Homes Fit for Heroes' campaign in Scotland. In 1935, the Scottish Architectural Advisory Committee commented on the outstanding quality of these developments and the likely importance of close central government supervision in producing these results:

> When the first post-War housing schemes were carried out under the Housing Act of 1919, the lay-out and type plans of the houses were required to be submitted to the Department for their formal approval before the work proceeded. It is true

that the houses erected under this Act were, generally speaking, more spacious in plan and less stereotyped in design than those erected under later Acts, but this does not altogether account for the superiority of their planning and detailed treatment over that of the majority of later schemes. The superiority must in some degree at least be ascribed to the detailed supervision of the plans by the Department.[1]

Sustaining the influence of garden city design proved difficult in Scotland during the 1920s and 1930s. As James Roxburgh had anticipated, in the prevailing Scottish conditions, it was going to be difficult to produce low density alternatives to the traditional working class tenements. Despite the generous subsidies provided for 1919 Act general needs housing, for reasons of affordability, the initial tenants were largely skilled industrial workers, small proprietors, and lower income white collar employees. These groups continued to benefit directly from local authority house building during the 1920s. As the supply of accommodation increased, and the costs of construction fell to more 'normal' levels, the focus of government policy shifted toward the removal of slum conditions and the reduction of severe overcrowding. In many respects this shift in priorities suited Scotland, and local authorities made vigorous use of the new legislation that emerged in the 1930s.

This transition, however, was not conducive to the expansion of garden city style housing for working class families in Scotland. During the 1930s local authorities were expected to provide new housing for much poorer tenants at a time of serious economic depression on a global scale. The pressures for austerity posed major constraints on density levels and standards of provision. In the event, tenement building was resumed in Scotland on a significant scale in order to respond to the rehousing needs of those displaced by local authority efforts to clear slums and relieve overcrowding.

1. Department of Health for Scotland, Report of the Scottish Architectural Advisory Committee (Edinburgh, 1935), p. 24.

SCOTTISH HOUSEBUILDING BETWEEN THE WARS

For Great Britain as a whole, the key trends in housing construction during the inter-war decades were a sharp decline in private sector building for rent and major increases in both local authority provision and speculative development for owner-occupation. In England and Wales, the dominant trend was the dramatic growth in speculative development for owner-occupation. In Scotland, however, the growth in local authority provision was dominant.

Between 1919 and 1939, on aggregate, 350,000 new dwellings were constructed in Scotland.[2] Of this number, two-thirds were built by local authorities and most of the remainder were provided by private developers. Although the level of demand for owner-occupation was fairly buoyant in the Edinburgh area during the 1930s, it was much less robust in other parts of Scotland.

2. Cole, *Building and Planning*, Table 1, p. 91.

Of the 240,000 properties constructed by Scottish local authorities during this period, 110,000 units were built for general needs and 130,000 units were associated with slum clearance schemes or other measures to relieve overcrowding. The level of output under the 1919 Act accounted for less than one-quarter of the provision for general needs. Nearly 70 per cent of the general needs stock was provided under the 1924 Housing Act, promoted by John Wheatley during his brief term as Minister of Health. Central government subsidies for general needs housing remained available in Scotland until 1933, although the vast proportion of this type of accommodation was completed and occupied by the end of the 1920s. Although a limited number of slum clearance schemes were carried out in Scotland during the 1920s, the bulk of the rehousing estates were built during the 1930s after the general supply of housing had expanded significantly.

With the shift in national priorities, Scottish local authorities responded by constructing as many as 50,000 units under the Housing Acts of 1930 and 1938 in order to rehouse those displaced by slum clearance schemes, and more than 60,000 units under the Housing Acts of 1935 and 1938 in order to relieve severe overcrowding.

CONTINUING INFLUENCES OF GARDEN CITY DESIGN

Throughout the 1920s, garden city influences were readily apparent in the design and layout of general needs housing built by Scottish local authorities. Once the 1919 Act funding provisions were withdrawn for reasons of economy, however, substantial reductions in internal space standards were imposed by central government. With the rising volume of local authority output under the Wheatley Act, the Scottish Board of Health found it difficult to maintain the detailed level of administrative supervision over various stages of the development process.[3] Many local authorities desired a greater degree of independence in their efforts to meet housing needs, and the cumbersome administrative controls were eventually relaxed substantially.[4]

As a rule, the Wheatley Act developments in Scotland are described as 'garden city' estates and this accommodation has also remained popular over the years. Unfortunately, the annual reports of the Scottish Board of Health did not include a statistical profile of the Wheatley Act stock built in Scotland, and consequently it is not possible to make any precise comparisons with the information presented in Chapter 6 for the 1919 Act stock. The Wheatley Act developments were substantially larger in scale, but the density levels were generally similar to those achieved under the 1919 Act. In terms of internal arrangements, very few of the Wheatley Act units were likely to contain a parlour and the amount of space within the living room and bedrooms were reduced significantly. In terms of architectural style, the Wheatley Act properties were more likely to be neo-Georgian in character given the central government pressures for economy and standardisation.

In relation to the speculative housing developments of the 1920s and 1930s, the Wheatley Act estates were more likely to embody garden city principles, particularly in providing community facilities and public open space for the benefit of local residents. Greater attention was also likely given to the grouping of properties to create a sense of variety and visually interesting streetscapes. As a rule, speculative developers opted for house types that were out of favour with garden city enthusiasts, such as detached bungalows and semi-detached cottages.

Within Scotland's larger cities and towns, the shifting priorities of the 1930s and the pressures for austerity in the face of economic depression made it difficult to continue the emphasis upon lower density forms of

3. Department of Health for Scotland, Report of the Scottish Architectural Advisory Committee, p. 24.
4. Ibid.

public sector provision. Nevertheless, in smaller settlements and rural villages where land costs were generally lower, it was still possible to produce interesting and attractive examples of working class housing in the garden city style. The contributions of two architects – Joseph Weekes and John A. W. Grant – were particularly impressive in keeping the garden city influence alive in Scotland during this period.

ARCHITECTURAL CONTRIBUTIONS OF JOSEPH WEEKES

Joseph Weekes (1881–1949) was a native of Edinburgh, who received his architectural training at Edinburgh College of Art.[5] He began his professional career in the Musselburgh practice of William Constable, and then was employed by the local authority in Fife as assistant burgh surveyor at Buckhaven. In 1910, he became burgh surveyor at Newport-on-Tay, and 5 years later took up a similar position at Irvine. After 2 years of military service during WW1, Weekes accepted an appointment as Housing Architect to Dunbarton County Council at the start of 1919, and was eventually promoted to County Architect in 1930. He remained in this post until his retirement from public service in 1947.

In his role as County Architect for Dunbartonshire, Weekes was responsible for a wide variety of building projects, including schools, police stations and health clinics. His earliest council housing developments, such as the 1919 Act properties at Alexandria in Wylie Avenue (see page 167), were built of red sandstone in an arts and crafts manner that was not overtly Scottish. According to John Gifford and Frank Walker, over the course of the 1920s and 1930s Weekes went on to develop an inventive and intimate approach that 'gave new expression to the Scottish vernacular tradition'.[6] His neo-vernacular developments usually incorporated traditional features, such as harled walls, doorways with moulded stone surrounds, crow-stepped gables and domed turrets, which are reminiscent of the earlier work by Robert Lorimer.[7]

During the 1930s, Weekes managed to produce an attractive range of local authority housing in various parts of West Dunbartonshire, at a time of financial austerity. For a number of these developments, his approach to the design of cottage flats was highly inventive and his

5. Biographical details for Joseph Weekes are drawn from two unpublished sources. One is a note prepared by David Whitham for a study visit to Dunbartonshire. The other is a joint dissertation submitted by two students at the Mackintosh School of Architecture in March 1980. Scott Greer and David Fulton were the authors of the dissertation titled Joseph Weekes, County Architect.
6. John Gifford and Frank Arneil Walker, Stirling and Central Scotland, Pevsner Architectural Guides (New Haven, 2002), p. 89.
7. Ibid.

ABOVE: Joseph Weekes (on the right, wearing a bow tie) at the unveiling of the Saltire Society plaque for his award winning Whyte's Corner development at Milton, Dunbartonshire, 1937. (Courtesy of the Archive Service, the Heritage Team, Culture and Creative Learning, West Dunbartonshire Council)

methods of arranging the properties around communal open spaces was suggestive of a garden city influence (especially the early work of Barry Parker and Raymond Unwin at New Earswick, Letchworth and Hampstead Garden Suburb). At first glance, these West Dunbartonshire developments seem to comprise 2-storey terraced cottages, but upon closer inspection they prove to consist mainly of cottage flats that are imaginatively positioned within complex 2-storey structures. In all probability, Weekes was aiming to demonstrate that economical forms of flatted accommodation could be created which were clearly superior to the free-standing 4-in-a-block cottage flats commonly built by local authorities across Scotland during the 1920s and 1930s.

At a more detailed level, Weekes' developments of cottage flats are seen to provide each household with a separate entrance door at ground level and an individual private garden, along with access to a common green or court designed to give a sense of place and community identity. His best known development of this type was built at Whyte's Corner in Milton in 1933 and later received a Saltire Society commendation in 1937.[8] A number of other examples were produced in 1938, in locations such as Old Kilpatrick (Hawcraigs), Rhu (Braehouse), Rosneath (Clachan Bridge) and Arrochar (Kirkfield Place). All of these developments appear to have retained their popularity as desirable places to live, and are now in mixed ownership as a result of Right-to-Buy purchases. Unfortunately, at the time of our site visit, the residents at Whyte's Corner in Milton and at Kirkfield Place in Arrocher were finding it difficult to co-ordinate external fabric repairs, a communal rather than an individual responsibility, for these outstanding flatted buildings.

ABOVE: Detail of Hawcraigs development of cottage flats at Old Kilpatrick. (Photo: John Reiach)

8. Charles McKean, *The Scottish Thirties* (Edinburgh, 1987), p. 145.

FACING PAGE

TOP: Whyte's Corner development of cottage flats at Milton. (Photo: John Reiach)

CENTRE: Another view of braehouse in the Dunbartonshire Village of Rhu, one of the outstanding 1930s local authority developments designed by County Architect Joseph Weekes. (Photo: John Reiach)

BOTTOM: Kirkfield Place development of cottage flats at Arrochar, now in mixed ownership and in evident need of external common repairs at the time of site visit. (Photo: John Reiach)

ARCHITECTURAL CONTRIBUTIONS OF JOHN A. W. GRANT

ABOVE: Unveiling of Saltire Society plaque for award winning houses designed by John A. W. Grant in the Westquarter development near Falkirk. (Courtesy of Falkirk Archives and Falkirk Community Trust)

John A. W. Grant (1885–1959) produced an impressive series of garden city developments for a variety of clients over the course of his professional career in architecture. He began his training as an apprentice in the Glasgow practice of Honeyman and Keppie. In 1912, he collaborated with Albert Gardener in winning a contract to design the co-partnership housing at Westerton Garden Suburb. Grant was primarily responsible for designing the housing and community facilities at Westerton in consultation with Raymond Unwin.

After WW1, Grant relocated to Edinburgh and set up his own independent practice. Three of his later projects are also notable examples of the continuing influence of garden city design in Scotland. In 1936, he won a competition for the design of Westquarter, a model village for miners to be constructed by Stirling County Council on a 120-acre site to the east of Falkirk. This development was intended to rehouse families that were living in substandard conditions within nearby mining villages. A total of 450 semi-detached houses and cottage flats were sensitively positioned to take advantage of the natural features

RIGHT: Cottage plans submitted by John A. W. Grant for post-WW1 design competition sponsored by the Local Government Board for Scotland and the Institute of Scottish Architects.

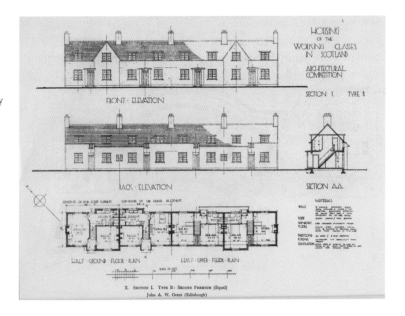

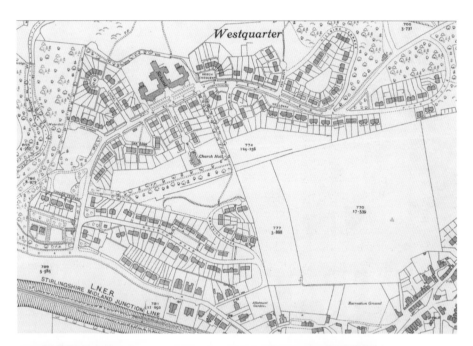

ABOVE: OS map of Westquarter near Falkirk, published in 1947. (Reproduced with the permission of the National Library of Scotland)

LEFT: Grouping of cottages in Laurel Grove, Westquarter designed by John A. W. Grant. (Photo: John Reiach)

of the site.[9] Additional provision was made at Westquarter for playing fields and local shops, as well as a village green, a school, a child welfare clinic and a recreation hall.[10] The entire project was awarded a Saltire Society commendation in 1939.

Also in 1939, John Grant designed a small development of local

9. Cmd. 5123, Seventh Annual Report of the Department of Health for Scotland, p. 28.

10. Ibid.

ABOVE: Salvesen Gardens, 1950s development for The Scottish Veterans' Garden City Association on the north side of Edinburgh in the Muirhouse area. (Photo: J. Rosser)

authority housing at Seafield Crescent, on the western edge of Dunbar in East Lothian. These 2-storey single-family cottages were linked in 3 groups to form an attractive symmetrical crescent. A total of 10 cottages were built in an arts and crafts manner, usually with 2 bedrooms each. These properties are comparable in quality to the best of the small developments built in Scotland under the 1919 Act, and since 1988 have had a listing of Category B.

Shortly after WW2, Grant designed a larger development of 70 cottages for The Scottish Veterans' Garden City Association known as Salvesen Gardens, within the Muirhouse area of Edinburgh. This accommodation consisted entirely of semi-detached properties and short terraces of 3 to 8 adjoining units, specially designed to meet the needs of severely injured service personnel. It seems a fitting example of the abiding influence of garden city design north of the Border.

1930s REVIVAL OF WORKING CLASS TENEMENT CONSTRUCTION

The shifting priorities of British housing policy in the 1930s had major implications for the built form of new council housing, especially in urban Scotland. Although various approaches were possible when dealing with slum conditions and extreme overcrowding, including the upgrading of existing properties, large scale demolition was usually the favoured course of action within larger cities and towns. Before any sizeable concentrations of derelict housing could be removed, the local authority now had a statutory obligation to ensure that suitable alternative accommodation was available for those displaced.

Similarly, in taking measures to relieve serious overcrowding, it was necessary to create an adequate supply of more spacious dwellings for rehousing purposes. Scotland's historic problem of overcrowding remained acute throughout the 1920s. The 1931 Census indicated that almost 17 per cent of all Scottish households were living in severely cramped conditions at a density of 3-or-more persons per room.[11] The corresponding figure for all English households was less than 2 per cent.[12]

Although the new 'rehousing estates' of the 1930s were usually built on suburban land, at densities well below the levels that had existed on central clearance sites, in the face of financial constraint it proved difficult to continue the construction of garden city style cottage housing. Typically, in the larger Scottish cities, the rehousing estates contained a mix of cottage flats and tenements, with few if any semi-detached or terraced single-family cottages. Where new tenements were provided on outlying sites they were normally built as 2- or 3-storey free standing pavilions in accordance with the recommendations of the Ballantyne Commission.

In 1933, the Department of Health for Scotland issued a publication titled *Housing of the Working Classes – Scotland, Economically Planned Houses of Satisfactory Design*.[13] Local authorities were advised to be mindful of the need for economy in building the required rehousing estates, in the interest of ratepayers and with a view to securing the lowest possible rents for the intended occupants.[14] The report included a selection of plans for various types of accommodation built under the 1924 and 1930 Housing Acts, which were regarded as successful examples of economic design. Although some of the recommended plans were for

11. Cmd. 4837, Sixth Annual Report of the Department of Health for Scotland, pp. 23-4.
12. Ibid.
13. Department of Health for Scotland, *Housing of the Working Classes – Scotland, Economically Planned Houses of Satisfactory Design* (Edinburgh, 1933).
14. Ibid., p. 3.

ABOVE: Key report issued by the Department of Health for Scotland in 1933, stressing the need for economy and highlighting desirable examples of cottage flats and pavilion-style tenements recent built by Scottish local authorities.

semi-detached and terraced cottages, the bulk of the material focused upon cottage flats and acceptable forms of pavilion-style tenements.

LIMITED IMPACT OF TOWN PLANNING SCHEMES

In the face of concerted pressure to meet official housebuilding targets during the 1920s ands 1930s, the rate of progress with town planning schemes was generally disappointing. This was particularly the case in Scotland. The town planning profession was at an early stage of development during this period, and both the supply of experienced personnel and the opportunities for professional training were very limited. As a consequence, the new suburban developments in both the public and private sectors were rarely planned as genuine garden suburbs with a full complement of civic and communal services, and in Scotland the attempts to create a full-scale garden city or satellite town had proved abortive.

Significant amendments to the statutory framework for town planning were included in the Town and Country Planning (Scotland) Act of 1932 and similar legislation for England and Wales. The key change in national policy was that formal town planning schemes could now be prepared for developed as well as undeveloped land.[15] This revision was intended to promote more effective strategies for the growth of city-regions and the regeneration of central areas, but the impact in Scotland was rather piecemeal during the remainder of the 1930s.

On the regional planning front, the Aberdeen and District Joint Town Planning Scheme was regarded as a significant achievement for its time. This scheme was jointly produced by Aberdeen Town Council, Aberdeen County Council, and Kincardine County Council and formally approved by the Department of Health for Scotland in March 1933 (shortly before the amended legislation came into operation).[16] The driving force behind this collaboration was Henry Alexander, Lord Provost of Aberdeen and a member of the Garden Cities and Town Planning Association.[17]

The Aberdeen and District Scheme was ambitious in scope, but it did not attempt to address any issues concerning the central areas of Aberdeen. In geographic terms, the scheme covered 62,000 acres

15. Cmd. 6552, Distribution of New Houses in Scotland, p. 12.
16. *Journal of the Town Planning Institute*, Vol. XX, No. 12, October 1934, pp. 337-8.
17. Ibid.

of outlying undeveloped land and put forward recommendations for the widening of existing roads, the construction of new roads, and the reservation of public and private open space within this catchment area. In addition, separate zones for residential and industrial development were designated for locations that warranted restrictions on the future pattern of land use. The final policy document received fulsome praise in Scottish town planning circles, from key figures such as William E. Whyte, G. D. Macniven, and Frank C. Mears.

The expanded powers for central area redevelopment strategies did highlight the need for slum clearance activities to be planned and implemented in a wider context, although little progress was achieved in practice before the end of the 1930s. At central government level in Scotland, however, an interesting policy review was undertaken to clarify whether height restrictions should be applied in cases where new tenements were to be built on slum clearance sites. Since the end of WW1, the Scottish Board of Health (and its successor body the Department of Health for Scotland) had generally been following the recommendations of the Ballantyne Commission regarding the desired form of any future tenement building.

Very few local authorities were carrying out slum clearance schemes during the 1920s, and the Ballantyne Commission recommendations were not widely questioned. One of the exceptions was Edinburgh, where the Town Council was committed to extending the gradual renewal approach in the Old Town originally promoted by Patrick Geddes in the 1880s and later adopted by the local authority in its area-based sanitary improvement scheme of 1893.[18]

In the early 1920s, Edinburgh Town Council decided to resume this approach in the heart of the Old Town, on designated sites within the Grassmarket and Canongate areas. City Architect Ebenezer J. MacRae proposed various in-fill developments of 4- and 5-storey stone built tenements on small clearance sites, which were regarded as appropriate forms of treatment for the regeneration of the medieval quarter.[19] Initially, these proposals were seriously questioned by central government officials, partly on the grounds that the new tenements would exceed the height limits recommended by the Ballantyne Commission. With strong backing from the Town Council, MacRae eventually gained approval for his original designs and these in-fill tenements have come to be recognised today as important early examples of sensitive physical

18. Johnson and Rosenburg, *Renewing Old Edinburgh – The Enduring Legacy of Patrick Geddes*, Chapters 3 and 4.

19. Ibid., Chapter 5.

ABOVE: 1930s linked pavilion-style tenements in West Richmond Street, Edinburgh designed by City Architect E. J. MacRae. (Photo: John Reiach)

20. Department of Health for Scotland, Report of the Scottish Architectural Advisory Committee.
21. Cmd. 4837, Sixth Annual Report of the Department of Health for Scotland, pp. 23-4.

regeneration within Edinburgh's UNESCO World Heritage Site.

During the 1930s, the Department of Health for Scotland organised various study visits to observe recent examples of higher density forms of housing. Official visits were made to England and the Continent. The party that travelled to Continental cities was led by John Highton, the Secretary to the Department of Health for Scotland. E. J. MacRae was an industrious member of the group, who was largely responsible for drafting the findings that appeared in a 1935 report titled *Working-class Housing on the Continent*. Also in 1935, other visits were made to sites of interest in central London, Liverpool and Manchester by members of the Scottish Architectural Advisory Committee. These findings appeared in a separate report concerned with 'architectural quality and amenity in the lay-out, planning and external treatment of houses for the working classes, and the erection of high tenements'.[20]

The Scottish Architectural Advisory Committee argued that the construction of 4- and 5-storey tenements should be permitted on central redevelopment sites, subject to consideration of factors such as orientation of the proposed housing, height and proximity of surrounding buildings, effects on adjacent existing buildings, sufficiency of light and air to the houses, and adequacy of open space provision.[21] Their report also recognised that a significant share of the population actually preferred to live in central locations, either because they enjoyed living in town or felt it was important to live near the workplace.[22] The case for relaxing the height restrictions for tenement building on inner-city clearance was accepted by the Department of Health for Scotland, although a 3-storey limit was generally maintained for local authority developments on outlying sites during the remainder of the 1930s.

SUSTAINING THE PRESSURES FOR REFORM IN SCOTLAND

The pre-1914 activities of the two Garden City Association branches in Scotland were discussed in Chapter 3. Once Britain was at war, both the Edinburgh & East of Scotland Branch and the Glasgow & West of Scotland Branch suspended operations and it appears that neither branch became active again. The Scottish Committee of the National Housing and Town Planning Council also ceased to function during WW1, and did not immediately resume its work once the war ended.

During the 1920s and 1930s, various measures were taken to sustain the momentum of the wider movement for housing reform, town planning and garden cities in Scotland. At the start of 1926, a meeting was held in Edinburgh with the aim of reconstituting the Scottish Committee of the National Housing and Town Planning Council as an independent body. Sir Henry Ballantyne agreed to serve as Honorary President and William E. Whyte took on the role of Secretary, in an effort to highlight the continuing urgency and distinctive character of Scotland's problems.[23]

Also in 1926, the Association for the Preservation of Rural Scotland was formed to focus greater attention on countryside issues. Among the leading members of this organisation were Sir John Stirling-Maxwell, who had been actively involved in the work of the Glasgow & West of Scotland Branch of the Garden City Association, and Frank Mears who had been collaborating with Patrick Geddes at home and abroad for nearly 20 years. Five years later, the Association for the Preservation of Rural Scotland played an important part in setting up the National Trust for Scotland.

Towards the end of 1929, various members of the Town Planning Institute put forward a proposal to form a Scottish Branch which was officially approved by the national body in February 1930.[24] The case for a Scottish Branch of the Town Planning Institute was made on the

22. Department of Health for Scotland, Report of the Scottish Architectural Advisory Committee, p. 14.

23. *Garden Cities & Town Planning*, Vol. XVI, No. 3, March 1926, p. 55.

grounds that Scotland had its own system of land tenure and a tradition of separate legislation in key policy areas. William Whyte, who had been a Legal Member of the Town Planning Institute for many years, played a key role in promoting the formation of the Scottish Branch.

In September 1937, another meeting was held in Glasgow to create a Scottish Branch of the Garden Cities and Town Planning Association, with William Whyte serving as President, Sir John Stirling-Maxwell serving as Vice-President and Jean Mann, a former Baillie of Glasgow Town Council, serving as Honorary Secretary.[25] In this instance, a Scottish Branch of the Garden Cities and Town Planning Association was regarded as essential to press for policy measures that responded effectively to the specific conditions found in Scotland. During the late 1930s and early 1940s, this body made an effort to assess the strengths and weaknesses of the inter-war experience in Scotland in order to clarify the desired direction of housing reform, town and country planning, and development of any new self-contained communities.

24. *Journal of the Town Planning Institute*, Vol. XVI, No. 5, March 1930, pp. 128-9.
25. *Town & County Planning – A Quarterly Review*, Vol. VI, No. 22, January 1938, p. 20.

SHAPING A FUTURE POLICY AGENDA FOR SCOTLAND

For long-time supporters of the garden city movement, the years of WW2 were partly a time to reflect on what should be done in the future. Scotland's legacy of poor housing conditions was still a huge problem, yet there was a growing sense that the recent emphasis on new housing provision had diverted attention away from other important issues. Many supporters of reform in Scotland were concerned about the lack of attention given to Scottish conditions in the Barlow Commission's final report on the location of industry and the distribution of population. Although William Whyte was a member of the Barlow Commission, and a substantial amount of evidence had been submitted on Scottish conditions, the final report published in 1940 contained only scant references to the current situation north of the Border.

A key submission to the Barlow Commission was made by a body named The Scottish Economic Committee, which had been appointed in 1936 to examine the potential for growth of light industries in Scotland. In 1939, The Scottish Economic Committee produced a publication titled *Scotland's Industrial Future – The Case for Planned Development*.

Among other things, the report discussed how the pattern of production during WW1 had affected the structure and performance of the Scottish economy. The relevant findings were as follows:

> The War... by creating new demands on Scottish heavy industries for armaments on a hitherto unprecedented scale, disturbed Scotland's economic and industrial equilibrium to an extent which has, twenty years after the Armistice, rendered recovery to the degree desirable a matter which should properly be regarded as of national concern.

> The whole force of the War economy, under the imperious stress of a struggle for existence, was directed towards exploiting Scotland's industrial and natural advantages for the production of armaments. There resulted an artificially inflated development in the heavy industries, which suffered, after the War, from the cessation of demand, depressed below customary levels by the Government's Disarmament programme. In other industries also the War had effected a considerable dislocation of trade, which had been diverted from its ordinary channels to the supply of military requirements. The result was that in many cases export markets were lost to Scottish industry, or at any rate the hold on them seriously weakened. It can scarcely be denied that the exigencies of war production have involved an obligation on the Government to restore the social balance of the Scottish industrial community, which was dislocated by the heavy demands made on the Naval and Military programme necessary for the successful prosecution of war.[26]

26. Scottish Economic Committee, *Scotland's Industrial Future – The Case for Planned Development*, pp. 18-9.
27. Jean Mann (ed.), *Replanning Scotland*, Town and Country Planning Association (Scotland), c. 1941.

ABOVE: Jean Mann, organiser of 1941 Largs Conference sponsored by the Scottish Branch of the Town and Country Planning Association. (Courtesy of the Archive Service, Glasgow Life, Mitchell Library, Glasgow)

In an effort to raise awareness of the evidence submitted to the Barlow Commission, the Scottish Branch of the Town and Country Planning Association (formerly known as the Garden Cities and Town Planning Association) organised a conference at Largs in early September 1941. The conference papers and proceedings were published in a book titled *Replanning Scotland*, edited by Jean Mann the organiser of this event.[27]

Jean Mann (1889–1964) had been an elected member of Glasgow Town Council from 1931 to 1938, during which time she served as Convenor of the Housing Committee. A strong advocate of garden cities and working class cottage provision, she also recognised that successful new communities would require more than well-designed houses. Jean Mann was later elected as the Labour Member of Parliament for Coatbridge in 1945.

Regardless of political affiliation, virtually all of the speakers at the Largs Conference stressed the importance of more effective forward planning at national, regional and local levels. Better co-ordination of industrial and residential development was seen to be a crucial issue in future policy development, as pointed out by Jean Mann in the preface to *Replanning Scotland*:

28. Ibid.

> Between the two wars... we did not build any new towns, but we built the *equivalent* in houses of 17 new towns, and threw up these houses around the perimeters of towns already too large, without regard to the convenience of the people, Industry, Transport, or our backward areas. The present municipally housed population [in effect] give their Housing Subsidy back to the transport companies, and their Trade Union benefits in reduced working hours are lost in travelling.[28]

Although a full-scale garden city had not been achieved in Scotland during the inter-war decades, a continuing need for new self-contained communities and satellite towns was generally recognised by the conference participants. For greater success in the future, a national strategy for the decentralisation of population and industry was seen as essential. The need to define appropriate forms of redevelopment for the central areas of major cities and larger towns was also acknowledged by a number of the speakers.

One of the keynote addresses at the Largs Conference was delivered by Frederic Osborn, who was then serving as Honorary Secretary of the Town and Country Planning Association. In his remarks to those assembled, he wisely refrained from any attempt to define the way forward for Scotland. Osborn used the occasion to reflect upon the early experience of the garden city movement, and made an impassioned plea for more balanced planning policies once Britain had again come through the ordeal of war. In recalling the pioneering days of the Garden City Association, he reminded the audience that:

...the Garden City idea... was looked upon as only one of the many idealistic fads. In fact nothing could be further from the truth. It was the first attempt to bring together all the things that really mattered and to synthesise them into an intelligent town building policy.[29]

29. F. J. Osborn, 'A balanced planning policy' in J. Mann (ed.), *Replanning Scotland*, p. 97.

Osborn also tried to counter the 'anti-urban' image of the garden city movement by stating his personal view that 'the town is essential to civilisation as we understand it and the vast majority of people believe in it and want it'. Although much has changed since the days of the Largs Conference, the quest for a more balanced planning approach has remained elusive and is now urgently required on a global scale.

Bibliography

Aalen, F. H. A. (1988), 'Homes for Irish heroes', *Town Planning Review*, 59 (3), pp. 305-23.

Aalen, F. H. A. (2002), 'English origins' in S. V. Ward, *The Garden City – Past, present and future*, London: E. & F. Spon, pp. 28-51.

Adams, I. H. (1978), *The Making of Urban Scotla*nd, London: Croom Helm. Aitken, P., C. Cunningham and B. McCutcheon (1984). *The Homesteads – Stirling's Garden Suburb*, Stirling: Privately printed.

Allan, C. E. and F. J. Allan (1916), *The Housing of the Working Classes Acts, 1890–1909 and the Housing Acts, 1914*, London: Butterworth & Co., Fourth edition.

Ballantine, W. M. (1944), *Rebuilding a Nation*, Edinburgh: Oliver and Boyd, Ltd.

Barrhead Community Council (1984), *Housing the Heroes*

Beattie, S. (1980), *A Revolution in London Housing*, London: The Architectural Press.

Begg, T. (1987), *50 Special Years – A Study in Scottish Housing*, London: Henry Melland.

Begg, T. (1996), *Housing Policy in Scotland*, Edinburgh: John Donald.

Bowley, M. (1945), *Housing and the State 1919–1944*, London: George Allen and Unwin Ltd.

Cd. 4016 (1908), Return shewing the Housing Conditions of the Population of Scotland.

Cd. 6192 (1912-13), Seventeenth Annual Report of the Local Government Board for Scotland.

Cd. 6720 (1913), Eighteenth Annual Report of the Local Government Board for Scotland.

Cd. 7327 (1914), Nineteenth Annual Report of the Local Government Board for Scotland.

Cd. 8041 (1914-16), Twentieth Annual Report of the Local Government Board for Scotland.

Cd. 8731 (1917), Report of the Royal Commission on the Housing of the Industrial Population of Scotland – Rural and Urban, Edinburgh: HMSO. (Ballantyne Commission Report)

Cd. 9191 (1918), Report of the Committee to Consider Questions of Building Construction in Connection with the Provision of Dwellings of the Working Classes in England and Wales, and Scotland, London: HMSO. (Tudor Walters Report)

Cd. 9197 (1918), Report of the Committee Appointed by the Minister of Reconstruction to Consider the Position of the Building Industry After the War, London: HMSO.

Cmd. 230 (1919), Twenty-fourth Annual Report of the Local Government Board for Scotland.

Cmd. 825 (1920), First Annual Report of the Scottish Board of Health. Cmd. 1319 (1921), Second Annual Report of the Scottish Board of Health. Cmd. 2156 (1924), Fifth Annual Report of the Scottish Board of Health.

Cmd. 2416 (1924-25), Sixth Annual Report of the Scottish Board of Health. Cmd. 4837 (1934), Sixth Annual Report of the Department of Health for Scotland.

Cmd. 5123 (1935), Seventh Annual Report of the Department of Health for Scotland.

Cmd. 6552 (1944), Distribution of New Houses in Scotland, Report by the Scottish Housing Advisory Committee, published by HMSO for the Department of Health for Scotland.

Bibliography

Co-partnership Tenants' Housing Council (1906), *Garden Suburbs, Villages, and Homes*,
   London: Co-partnership Tenants' Housing Council.

Co-partnership Tenants' Housing Council (1912), *Garden Suburbs, Villages, and Homes*, No. 2,
   London: Co-partnership Tenants' Housing Council.

Cole, G. D. H. (1945), *Building and Planning*, London: Cassell and Company, Ltd.

Corporation of Glasgow (1927), Housing Department – Review of Operations from 1919
   to 1927, Glasgow: Corporation of Glasgow.

Cramond, R. D. (1966), *Housing Policy in Scotland 1919–1964*, University of Glasgow Social
   and Economic Studies Research Papers No. 1, Edinburgh: Oliver and Boyd.

Culpin, E. G. (1914), *Garden City Movement Up-to-Date*, London: Garden Cities and
   Town Planning Association.

Cumming, E. (2006), *Hand, Heart and Soul*, Edinburgh: Birlinn Ltd.

Daunton, M. J. (1983), *House and Home in the Victorian City*, London: Edward Arnold.

Daunton, M. J. (1983), 'Public place and private space: the Victorian city and the working-class
   household' in D. Fraser and A. Sutcliffe, *The Pursuit of Urban History*,
   London: Edward Arnold, pp. 212-33.

Department of Health for Scotland (1933), *Housing of the Working Classes –*
   Scotland, Economically Planned Houses of Satisfactory Design, Edinburgh: HMSO.

Department of Health for Scotland (1933), Report of the Scottish Departmental
   Committee on Housing, Edinburgh: HMSO.

Department of Health for Scotland (1935), Report of the Scottish Architectural
   Advisory Committee, Edinburgh: HMSO.

Department of Health for Scotland (1935), *Working-class Housing on the Continent*,
   Edinburgh: HMSO.

East Dunbartonshire County Council (2011), Westerton Garden Suburb Conservation
   Area Appraisal, Draft January 2011.

Edwards, A. T. (1913), 'A criticism of the garden city movement', Town Planning Review,
   Vol. IV, No. 2, pp. 150-7.

Edwards, A. T. (1914), 'A further criticism of the garden city movement', *Town Planning Review*,
   Vol. IV, No. 4, pp. 312-18.

Fraser, M. (1996), *John Bull's Other Houses*, Liverpool: Liverpool University Press.

Frew, J. (1985), *Fit Habitations*, St Andrews: Crawford Centre for the Arts.

Frew, J. (1987), *Housing the Heroes*, Kirkcaldy: Kirkcaldy District Council.

Frew, J. (1989), ''Homes fit for heroes: early municipal house building in Edinburgh',
   Journal of the Architectural Heritage Society Scotland, No. 16, pp. 26-37.

Frew, J. (1991), 'Ebenezer MacRae and reformed tenement design 1930 – 1940' in J. Frew and
   D. Jones (eds.), *Scotland and Europe, Proceedings of a Symposium Held at The
   University, St Andrews May 19th 1990*.

Frew, J. (1997), 'Cottages, tenements and 'practical' idealism: James Thomson at Logie, 1917–1923' in D. Mays (ed.), *The Architecture of Scottish Cities*, East Linton: Tuckwell Press, pp. 171-79.

Frew, J. (2000), 'Towards a municipal housing blueprint: the architects' panel competition and its aftermath 1918–1919', *Architectural Heritage* XI, pp. 43-54.

Frew, J. and Adshead, D. (1987), 'Model' colliery housing in Fife: Dunbeath Garden Village, 1904–1908', *Scottish Industrial History*, v. 10.1 and 10.2, pp. 45-59.

Gaskell, S. M. (1981), 'The suburb salubrious: town planning in practice' in A. Sutcliffe (ed.), *British Town Planning: The formative years*, Leicester: Leicester University Press, pp. 16-61.

Geddes, P. (1910), 'The civic survey of Edinburgh' in *Royal Institute of British Architects, Transactions of Town Planning Conference – London, 10-15 October 1910*, London: Royal Institute of British Architects, pp. 537-74.

Geddes, P. (1968), *Cities in Evolution*, London: Ernest Benn Ltd.

Gifford, J. and Walker, F. A. (2002), *Stirling and Central Scotland*, New Haven: Yale University Press.

Gleave, S. (1987), The Influence of the garden city movement in Fife, 1914–23, Unpublished M. Phil., University of St Andrews.

Glendinning, M., MacInnes, R. and MacKechnie, A. (1996), *A History of Scottish Architecture*, Edinburgh: Edinburgh University Press.

Glendinning, M. (1997), 'The Ballantyne report: a "1917 revolution" in Scottish housing' in D. Mays (ed.), *The Architecture of Scottish Cities*, East Linton: Tuckwell Press, pp. 161-70.

Glendinning, M. (2003). 'Tenements and flats' in G. Stell, J. Shaw and S. Storrier, *Scotland's Buildings*, East Linton: Tuckwell Press, pp. 108-26.

Grier, S. and D. Fulton (1980), 'Joseph Weekes, County Architect', Unpublished dissertation, Mackintosh School of Architecture, Glasgow School of Art.

Hamilton, T. W. (1947), *How Greenock Grew*, Greenock: James McKelvie & Sons Ltd.

Hardy, D. (1991), *From Garden Cities to New Towns: Campaigning for Town and Country Planning*, London: Routledge.

Hardy, D. (1992), 'The garden city campaign: an overview' in S. V. Ward, *The Garden City – Past, present and future*, London: E. & F. Spon, pp. 187-209.

Harrison, J. G. (1998), 'Wooden-fronted houses and forestairs in early modern Scotland', *Architectural Heritage* IX, pp. 71-83.

Horsfall, T. C. (1904), *The Improvement of Dwellings and Surroundings of the People: The Example of Germany*, Manchester: Manchester University Press. Howard, E. (1902), *Garden Cities of Tomorrow*, London: Swan Sonnenschein & Co. Ltd., Third edition.

Bibliography

Hughes, M. (ed.) (1972), *The Letters of Lewis Mumford and Frederic J. Osborn: A Transatlantic Dialogue 1938-70*, New York: Praeger.

Johnson, J. and L. Rosenburg (2010), *Renewing Old Edinburgh – The Enduring Legacy of Patrick Geddes*, Glendaruel: Argyll Publishing.

Johnson, B. P. (1968), *Land Fit for Heroes*, Chicago & London: University of Chicago Press.

Kay, S. (2014), *Homes for Welsh Workers*, Abergavenny: 325 Press.

Leneman, L. (1989), *Fit for Heroes?*, Aberdeen: Aberdeen University Press.

Lenman, B. and W. D. Carroll (1972), 'Council housing in Dundee', *Town Planning Review*, Vol. 43, No. 3, pp. 275-85.

Local Government Board (1919), *Manual on the Preparation of State-Aided Housing Schemes*, London: HMSO.

Local Government Board for Scotland (1918), *Provision of Houses for the Working Classes after the War*, Edinburgh: HMSO.

Local Government Board for Scotland (1918), Report of the Women's House-Planning Committee, Edinburgh: HMSO.

Local Government Board for Scotland (1919), *Housing of the Working Classes in Scotland*, Edinburgh: HMSO.

London County Council (1913), *Housing of the Working Classes in London*, London: London County Council.

McKean, C. (1987), *The Scottish Thirties*, Edinburgh: Scottish Academic Press Ltd.

McWilliam, C. (1975), *Scottish Townscape*, London: Collins.

MacPherson, A. (1860), Report of a Committee of the Working-Classes of Edinburgh on the Present Overcrowded and Uncomfortable State of their Dwelling Houses, Edinburgh: Paton & Ritchie.

Mairet, P. (1957), *Pioneer of Sociology*, London: Lund Humphries.

Mann, J. (ed.) (c. 1941), *Replanning Scotland*, Glasgow: Town and Country Planning Association (Scotland).

Marsh, J. (1982), *Back to the Land*, London: Quartet Books Ltd.

Meacham, S. (1999), *Regaining Paradise*, New Haven and London: Yale University Press.

Meller, H. (1990), *Patrick Geddes: Social Evolutionist and Town Planner*, London: Routledge.

Melling, J. (1989), 'Clydeside rent struggles and the making of Labour politics in Scotland, 1900-39' in R. Rodger (ed.), *Scottish Housing in the Twentieth Century*, Leicester: Leicester University Press, pp. 54-88.

Miller, M. (1981), 'Raymond Unwin 1863-1940' in G. E. Cherry (ed.), *Pioneers in British Planning*, London: The Architectural Press, pp. 72-102.

Miller, M. (1992), *Raymond Unwin: Garden Cities and Town Planning*, Leicester: Leicester University Press.

Miller, M. (2010), *English Garden Cities*, Swindon: English Heritage.

Minett, J. (1989), 'Government sponsorship of new towns: Gretna 1915–17 and its
implications' in R. Rodger (ed.), *Scottish Housing in the Twentieth Century*, Leicester:
Leicester University Press, pp. 104-24.

Morgan, N. J. (1989), '"£8 cottages for Glasgow citizens" – Innovations in municipal house
building in Glasgow in the inter-war years' in R. Rodger (ed.) *Scottish Housing in the
Twentieth Century*, Leicester: Leicester University Press, pp. 125-54.

Murray, J. B. (1995), *Stoneyburn: The Forgotten Baby*, Wellpark: West Lothian District Council.
'New Townsmen' (1918), *New Towns after the War*, London: J. M. Dent & Sons Ltd.

Osborn, F. J. (1938), *Evidence of the Garden Cities and Town Planning Association Given to the
Barlow Royal Commission on the Geographic Distribution of the Industrial Population*,
London: Garden Cities and Town Planning Association.

Osborn, F. J. (1950), 'Sir Ebenezer Howard – The Evolution of his Ideas', *The Town Planning
Review*, Vol. XXI, No. 3, 221-235.

Osborne, B. D. (1980), 'Dumbarton shipbuilding and workers' housing 1850–1900', *Scottish
Industrial History*, Vol. 3.1, pp. 2-9.

Parker, B. and R. Unwin (1901), *The Art of Building a Home*, London: Longmans, Green & Co.

Pepper, S. and M. Swenarton (2008), 'Home fronts' in M. Swenarton,
Building the New Jerusalem, Bracknell: IHS BRE Press, pp. 13-28.

Pepper, S and M. Swenarton (2008), 'Neo-Georgian maison-type' in M. Swenarton,
Building the New Jerusalem, Bracknell: IHS BRE Press, pp. 29-40. Reid, A. (2000),
Brentham – A History of the Pioneer Garden Suburb 1901–2001,
London: Brentham Heritage Society.

Robertson, D., J. Smyth and I. McIntosh (2008), 'The Raploch: A history, people's
perceptions and the likely future of a problem housing estate',
Architectural Heritage XIX, pp. 83-97.

Robins, N. A. (1992), *Homes for Heroes*, Swansea: Swansea City Council. Robinson, P. J. (1984),
'Tenements: a pre-industrial urban tradition', *ROSC Review of Scottish Culture*, No.
1, pp. 52-64. Robinson, P. J. (1986), 'Tenements: the industrial legacy', *ROSC Review
of Scottish Culture*, No. 2, pp. 71-83.

Rodger, R. (1983), 'The invisible hand – market forces, housing and the urban form in
Victorian cities' in D. Fraser and A. Sutcliffe (eds.), *The Pursuit of Urban History*,
London: Edward Arnold, pp. 190-211.

Rodger, R. (1983), The evolution of Scottish town planning' in G. Gordon and B. Dicks (eds.),
Scottish Urban History, Aberdeen: Aberdeen University Press, pp. 71-91.

Rodger, R. (1986), 'The Victorian building industry and the housing of the Scottish working
class' in M. Doughty (ed.), *Building the Industrial City*, Leicester: Leicester
University Press, pp. 152-206.

Bibliography

Rodger, R. (1995), *Housing in Urban Britain, 1780–1914,*,
    Cambridge: Cambridge University Press.

Rodger, R. (1996), 'Urbanisation in twentieth-century Scotland' in T. M. Devine and
    R. J. Finlay (eds.), *Scotland in the 20th Century*, Edinburgh: Edinburgh
    University Press, pp. 122-52.

Rodger, R. (1999), 'Building development' in M. Glendinning and D. Watters (eds.),
    Home Builders – MacTaggart & Mickel and the Scottish Housebuillding Industry,
    Edinburgh: RCAHMS, pp. 193-210.

Rodger, R. (2011), *Edinburgh's Colonies*, Glendaruel: Argyll Publishing. Roxburgh, J. F. (1912),
    'Town-planning in Scotland: the tenement problem', *The Blue Blanket – An
    Edinburgh Civic Review*, No. 4, pp. 316-26.

Royal Institute of British Architects (1918), *Cottage Designs*, London:
    Royal Institute of British Architects.

Russell, J. B. (1905), 'On the immediate results of the operations of the Glasgow
    Improvement Trust at May, 1874' in A. K. Chalmers (ed.), *Public Health
    Administration in Glasgow*, Glasgow: James Maclehose and Sons, pp. 96-113.

Scottish Economic Committee (1939), *Scotland's Industrial Future –
    The Case for Planned Development*, Scottish Economic Committee Publication.

Scottish Housing Advisory Committee (1948), *Planning Our New Homes*, Edinburgh: HMSO.

Sharp, T. (1932), *Town and Countryside*, London: Oxford University Press.

Sharp, T. (1940), *Town Planning*, Harmondsworth: Penguin Books Ltd.

Simpson, M. (1985), *Thomas Adams and the Modern Planning Movement*, London: Mansell.

Skilleter, K. J. (1993), '*The role of public utility societies in early British town planning and
    housing reform*', *Planning Perspectives*, 8, pp. 125-65. Sutcliffe, A. (1981),
    Towards the Planned City, Oxford: Basil Blackwell.

de Soissons, M. (1988), *Welwyn Garden City: A Town Designed for Healthy Living*,
    Cambridge: Publications for Companies.

Swenarton, M. (1981), *Homes fit for Heroes*, London: Heinemann Educational Books.

Swenarton, M. (1989), *Artisans and Architects*, Basingstoke and London: Macmillan.

Tarn, J. N. (1973), *Five Per Cent Philanthropy*, Cambridge: Cambridge University Press.

Thompson, W. (1899), *Housing of the Working Classes*, Richmond, Surrey: Borough of Richmond.

Tims, M. (1966), *Ealing Tenants Ltd*, London: Ealing Local History Society,
    Members' Papers, No. 8.

Unwin, R. (1907), 'Cottage planning' in *First Garden City Ltd, Where Shall I Live?*,
        London: First Garden City Ltd, pp. 103-9.

Unwin, R. (1909), *Town Planning in Practice*, London: T. Fisher Unwin Ltd.

Vivian, H. (1912), 'Garden cities, housing and town-planning', *The Quarterly Review*,
        Vol. 216, pp. 493-515.

Walker, F. A. (1982), 'The Glasgow Grid', in T. A. Markus (ed.),
        Order and Space in Society, Edinburgh: Mainstream Publishing, pp. 155-200.

Ward, S. V. (1994), *Planning and Urban Change*, London: Paul Chapman Publishing Ltd.

Ward, S. V. (2002), 'The Howard legacy' in K. C. Parsons and D. Schuyler (eds.),
        From Garden City to Green City, Baltimore and London: Johns Hopkins
        University Press, pp. 222-44.

Westerton Women's Group (1993), *Westerton – A Village Story*,
        Glasgow: Westerton Women's Group.

Wheatley, J. (1913), *Eight Pound Cottages for Glasgow Citizens*, Glasgow: Glasgow Labour Party.

Whitelaw, M. (1992), *A Garden Suburb for Glasgow: The Story of Westerton*,
        Glasgow: Privately printed.

Whitham, D. (1989), 'State Housing and the Great War' in R. Rodger (ed.),
        Scottish Housing in the Twentieth Century,
        Leicester: Leicester University Press, pp. 89-103.

Whyte, W. E. (1920), *Housing: The Growth of State Interest and Control*,
        Edinburgh and Glasgow: William Hodge and Company.

Whyte, W. E. (1934), *Town and Country Planning in Scotland*,
        Edinburgh and Glasgow: William Hodge and Company.

Williams, N. J. (2000), 'Housing' in W. H. Fraser and C. H. Lee (eds.),
        Aberdeen 1800–2000, East Linton: Tuckwell Press, pp. 295-322.

Index

Index

Index